Acknowledgement
The publishers wish to thank the Lone Pine Koala Sanctuary, the Port of Echuca, Swan Hill Pioneer Settlement and the National Trust of Australia (Victoria), for their kind assistance.

Texts by Joe Ryan and Rupert O. Matthews
First published in Great Britain 1984 by Colour Library Books Ltd.

Display and text filmsetting by Acesetters Ltd., Richmond, Surrey, England.
Colour separations by Llovet S.A., Barcelona, Spain.
Printed and bound in Barcelona, Spain by Rieusset and G. Estella.

ISBN 0 86283 159 8

AUSTRALIA
The Timeless Continent

Produced by
Ted Smart & David Gibbon

Featuring the Photography of
Neil Sutherland
Eberhard Streichan & Øystein Klakegg

Published by Colour Library Books for
GORDON & GOTCH LTD

Australia is an enormous land. Here, a man can stand and look from one horizon to the other, from one year's end to another and never see another human being. The vast reaches of arid land in the outback may see a plume of dust kicked up as a vehicle travels the long, lonely miles between stations. Or the bush may echo to the roar of a chain saw. But the endless horizons are largely untouched by civilisation and industry. There are vast stretches of outback and bush where no white man has trodden to this very day, but the Aborigines have been there.

According to the original inhabitants of this continent nation, the land had its origins in the magical Dreamtime: a time when Nurunderi strode the land in search of his wives; a time when the sticks of the sky people burst into flame and created the sun. During this time of gods, animal spirits and fabulous ancestors the world was created amid violent passions and quarrels.

The white man, a newcomer to these shores, has a more prosaic, and probably more accurate, account of the formation of the continent. As the molten surface of the primeval planet cooled it formed great chunks of rock that are today's continents. Australia was one of these. It seems that some 200 million years ago Australia was linked with the other continents of the southern hemisphere in the super-continent of Gondwanaland. But some time during the 'Age of the Dinosaurs', the Mesozoic Era, Gondwanaland broke up and Australia drifted away into quiet isolation that was to last for millions of years.

It is often said that Australia is the world's oldest continent. This is obviously not true, for all the continents were formed at about the same time, some 4,000,000,000 years ago. What is true, however, is that Australia contains some of the oldest rocks in the world, some 3,000,000,000 years old, which outcrop in Western Australia. The continent has remained, geologically, remarkably stable and peaceful for an immense period of time. The titanic forces that raised the Rocky Mountains and the Alps, indeed all the major mountains of the world, passed Australia by. The most recent Australian mountains were thrown up in the late Palaeozoic era, long before even the dinosaurs walked the earth. The weathered stumps of these mountains form the Great Dividing Range of the present day. The immense length of time during which little has happened has made Australia a land of low relief and few mountains. In fact only some six per cent of the land is over 2,000 feet in altitude and the maximum height of 7,316 feet is dwarfed by that of all the other continents.

The mountainous island state of Tasmania stands like a sentinel in the raging seas south of the mainland. The attraction of the land lies in its diversity and character. The rich orchards of the historic Huon Valley make a pleasant contrast to the wilds of the mountains and west coast. Here, the dreaded horizontal – a small, densely growing tree – bars any exploration from the ground by even the most experienced bushwhacker. It is in these hidden lands that the Tasmanian wolf is thought still to survive, far away from the intrusions of modern man. The jagged peaks of the mountains tower majestically above the lakes that are such a feature of the central plateau region. The great eucalyptus forests and scrubland make up a unique area of great natural beauty where marsupials and native birds flourish.

Across the Bass Strait lies the state of Victoria, which has been aptly named the Garden State for, despite the fires, it is one of the most fertile and pleasant regions in the nation. Reaching into the skies are the smooth ridges of the Southern Alps. In the winter the snow-covered peaks create a fairyland of glistening snow and ice, where crystal icicles hang from the branches. The foothills of these mountains are rolling, scenic landscapes; a wonderland at any time of the year.

As well as some of the densest forest on the continent, Victoria has vast areas of mallee. The open eucalyptus scrubland once covered far more land than now, since much has been cleared and is now farmed for grain. The mallee may not be as scenically beautiful as the mountains, but it is fascinating nonetheless. The wildlife that scurries around in the undergrowth includes wallabies, roos and emus, as well as the unique mallee fowl.

Previous pages the Olgas.
Facing page and overleaf koalas.

The mighty Murray River flows westwards across the landscape, bringing life-giving moisture to the land. Beyond the tumbling waters of Australia's greatest river, beyond the rich orchards and farmlands of Riverina, beyond the black stump itself, stretch the wide pastoral lands that are the basis of the nation's animal wealth. The seemingly endless grasslands stretch away to the horizon in all directions. The lonely visitor is left with a feeling of his own insignificance set against the sheer scale of nature's vastness. The verdant landscape is only broken by the sheep and the station worker mustering his charges for shearing. Some 70 million sheep are sheared in the area every year, but even this number can seem lost in the sweeping land.

The great tracts of grazing land reach eastwards to the foothills of the Great Dividing Range and westwards to the edge of the great deserts. Northwards, the land runs on across the Darling Downs, west of Brisbane, into the hot, tropical land of Queensland. On the other side of the Great Dividing Range the landscape is one of fertile ground and luxurious, sandy beaches until the dramatic Glasshouse Mountains are reached. These sheer plugs of volcanic rock that rise so suddenly from the plains are the remains of violent eruptions that shook the region millions of years ago. The central vents of the volcanoes became clogged with molten magma which then solidified. As the surrounding cone eroded, the vertical plug was left standing free.

Along the northeast coast of the continent, east of the Great Dividing Range, lie stretches of steamy tropical rainforest. The lush greenery of the rainforest is dependent upon the regular dousing that comes with each tremendous downpour. In such a humid climate the rate of growth of the plants is phenomenal. In the race to survive many plants use ingenious and sinister methods. The pitcher plants will lure insects to the edge of the pitcher by exuding nectar, then trap and digest them in a secreted enzyme. The strangling fig grows around the trunk of a host tree, eventually destroying it.

Off the sultry coast lies one of nature's wonders: the Great Barrier Reef. This tropical wonderland of colourful fish and rich sealife is based upon the coral reef itself, which lies some miles offshore. The reef is composed of the remains of thousands of generations of tiny animals, but it is its size that is so staggering. For more than 2,000 kilometres the crashing surf of the Pacific throws its spray high into the air over the jagged points of the reef. The coral reaches the surface, where it is bathed in the strong sunlight, and in places plunges some 70 metres into the dark depths to the sea floor. In and out of the cracks and crevices of the coral formations swim and crawl starfish, lobsters, angel fish, turtles and a whole host of other strange and exotic species. Across the 207,000 square kilometres of the reef's area there are many hundreds of idyllic tropical islands. Many of these have become popular resorts with Australians as they chase the sun.

Cape York is generally difficult to travel through, indeed, for the average traveller it is all but impossible. The combination of steep escarpments, plunging chasms and broad rivers, not to mention the almost complete lack of roads, put it beyond the reach of all but the most determined and experienced. The impenetrable, swampy jungles of northern Cape York make a fitting end to one of the wildest and most beautiful regions of the country. The vast area of land north of Mossman is populated only by the inhabitants of a few mining settlements and Aboriginal communities. It is surely one of the last great, untamed wildernesses left on earth.

During the dry season the few roads and tracks of the area make for exciting four-wheel motoring. But during the 'Big Wet' the few roads and many fords are completely impassable as untamed nature takes over and undoes the work of man. To the southwest the murky mangrove swamps around the Gulf of Carpentaria have always defied the attempts of man to explore their interior. The sticky, shifting mud and close-growing stems and roots have made the area inaccessible to civilisation.

In contrast, the great stretches of the Channel Country to the south are forbidding for their very dryness. In this land of endless horizons the dust from the traveller's boots is the only moving

Facing page a kookaburra.

thing visible amid the scrub and dirt. But the flat, arid lands undergo a startling change when the waters come. It does not actually rain in the Channel Country. The water pours down the Cooper, Georgina and Hamilton as the clouds burst far to the north. Millions of gallons of water tumble across the arid plains, rushing south in their attempt to reach Lake Eyre. But the desert heat and water holes account for every drop of moisture before it can reach the great salt lakes. Following the water is a profusion of greenery and floral splendour that makes the desert seem a veritable paradise. Animals, both wild and domestic, come in their thousands to feed on the lush pasture before the burning sun withers it into dust again.

Despite the terrible heat and burning sun of the interior the waters that gush across the sands sometimes actually reach the great salt lakes. On occasional years a trickle of water will run into the lake beds and moisten them, but in 1950 the rains that fell far to the north were nothing short of tremendous. Raging floods gushed across the Channel Country and by the spring of 1950 some 8,000 square kilometres of Lake Eyre were under water. The influx of water dissolved the 400 million tonnes of salt and the vast area of water became as salty as the sea. Fish appeared and survived for some time before the water evaporated in the scorching heat and the lake reverted to its normal, desolate self. Another of the empty lakes, Lake Yamma Yamma, is remarkable for its flat shores. When it has water in it, a steady wind can shift the position of the lake considerably.

South of Lake Eyre is the town of Maree, the start of the Birdsville Track. This famous stock track winds across the interior to Birdsville in Queensland and was once an important trade route. West of Maree, beyond Woomera, stretch the great expanses of the Nullarbor. This mighty, 260,000 square kilometre desert is underlain by a plateau of limestone, which accounts, in part, for its appearance and its name. The underlying rock is remarkably flat and it is this that gives the unique, endless flatness to the area, while the thin soil that it has produced accounts for the vegetation. Unable to hold moisture or deep roots, the soil has imposed a herbaceous growth on the land. No tree or even large shrub can gain a foothold and only small plants with a shallow root system manage to survive. In turn this has given the desert its name, which derives from *nullus arbor*, Latin for 'no tree'.

For many years this great expanse of burning, shadeless waste was an almost unassailable block to communications. Today, however, there is both a road and a rail link across the 'no-tree' desert. The railway includes the longest stretch of straight track in the world; some 483 kilometres of it. Between Eucla and Bookabie the Eyre Highway runs close to the Cliffs of the Nullarbor, where the limestone plateau plunges from a dizzying height to the crashing surf of the Great Australian Bight. It was in this stretch of sea that Matthew Flinders lost his anchors in 1803.

Across the Nullarbor and beyond the gold-rich desert towns of Kalgoorlie and Coolgardie is the fertile southwest around Perth and Albany. Vast areas of the region have been given over to cereal growing. Between Geraldton and Albany is a great sweep of golden grain fields, waving in the sparkling sunlight as the soft breeze stirs the ears. Some two million hectares of Western Australia's finest land is given over to the production of crops, while much of the rest is pastureland.

This fertile area has been separated from the rest of the island continent by great stretches of desert to the north and east for thousands of years. Being isolated from a continent that was itself isolated from the rest of the world has had a profound effect on the flora of the region. The rugged mountains of the Stirling Range and Porongurups rise above majestic stands of karri and tingle. The tree trunks rise sheer, like smooth pillars, to the canopy far above and some giants may reach a height of fully 60 metres. But it is the less dramatic plants that are the more impressive by their sheer beauty and overwhelming numbers.

In the spring, vast areas of land become carpeted with shades of colour of every description as millions upon millions of flowers burst their buds. There are some three thousand species of

Facing page a kangaroo.

wild flower in the area south of the Murchison River and the vast majority of them are found nowhere else on earth; a legacy of the region's isolation. The arresting scarlet of the bottlebrushes shines out from the depths of the bush as the delicate blooms bob in the breeze. The yellow or red banksias hold their bright cylinders high to the sun, seeming so alien to the drab shrub that produces them. Further north, as the land becomes more arid, the ephemerals take over the landscape. Brought to life by the infrequent showers of the region, mulla mullas and everlastings erupt from the bare soil and carpet it with a sea of colour. Of all these desert ephemerals, perhaps the best known and most colourful is Sturt's Desert Pea, whose scarlet and black blooms can be found right across the arid interior of the continent.

The land further north may be less inviting, but the scenic beauty of the land increases to the truly spectacular. Standing like soldiers on parade on the sandy desert floor are the Pinnacles; a bizarre, almost unearthly formation created by the trunks of long-petrified trees being exposed amid the sand.

Beyond the Gascoyne River, which actually flows a few feet beneath the river bed, stretch the Pilbara and the Hammersley Range. Intermittent streams, often only metres wide, have carved plunging canyons from the richly coloured rock. The walls of the chasms, which may tower for a hundred metres, are made up of a myriad hues that darken or glow in the sunlight. Dales Gorge is over 45 kilometres long and contains the magnificent Fortesque Falls. The streams that have cut such glorious features into the earth only flow when there has been rain, but along their courses billabongs hold the water throughout the year. At Millstream, thousands of birds swoop down to drink the thirst-quenching water that is the clearest for miles, and in so doing make a magnificent show amid the rushes and ferns.

The Kimberley region lies in the north, bordering the Timor Sea, and is an area of rugged beauty and scenery. Near Halls Creek are two natural curiosities. The first is a crater some 850 metres across and 60 metres deep, marking the spot where a massive meteorite smashed into the earth a million years ago. The second is a white stone wall that looks man made. In fact, it is a vertical seam of quartz that has eroded more slowly than the surrounding soft rock and has been left standing free.

The coast around Arnhem Land is one of dense mangrove swamps and thick, sticky mud. Behind the impenetrable mass of mangroves lies a forest of distinctly-tropical and almost Malaysian character. The weather is uncomfortably warm and wet for most of the year, with rainfall of over 2 metres not unusual. Further south the climate becomes progressively drier as the effects of the monsoon peter out. The forests and crocodile-infested rivers first give way to open forest land and then to the valuable pastureland of the Barkly Tableland.

But it is far to the south that the heart and focus of the great, untamed Australian outback is to be found: the Red Centre.

Vast seas of shifting red sands march across the landscape for hundreds of miles in dunes up to 40 metres high. The great Simpson Desert covers 145,000 square kilometres of the Centre and swallows up the Todd and Hay rivers in its burning, arid depths. The symmetrical ridges of the great MacDonnell Ranges run to the horizons and are cut by majestic chasms. Here the dancing sunlight plays on the water surface and scatters in a myriad bouncing lights on the burning red walls of the canyons. Strange and wonderful rock formations shelter the weird wildlife that scampers around in the shadows; lizards with fearsome frills and reptiles with spikes like some nightmare monster.

All this grandeur, magnificence and desolation revolves around one spot. At the heart of the Red Centre, and the heart of the continent, stands the gigantic Ayers Rock. Rising above the flat, featureless landscape like a monstrous behemoth, the Rock surveys the creation around it. In its untamed bulk, it signifies the wildness and beauty that is Australia.

Facing page a red kangaroo. *Overleaf* Ayers Rock

LENNONS
MLC
MLC
ANN ST
ALBERT ST

When the colony of Queensland became independent in 1859, there were only a few pence in the treasury! Today, its sub-tropical capital, Brisbane, reflects the growing affluence of the state and acts as its 'sunny gateway'.

Looking down from Mount Coot-tha, 8 kilometres south-west of the city centre, one can see Brisbane spread out below. Australia's third largest city, it lies astride the Brisbane River which winds its way out to Moreton Bay, 19 kilometres down-stream. In 1821, the Surveyor-General, John Oxley, began exploring the land north of the Liverpool Plains looking for suitable sites for prison camps. In 1824 he arrived with convicts and troops at Redcliffe, but the hostile Aborigines and lack of fresh water caused him to move south to Edenglassie. When this convict settlement was declared a town in 1834, it was renamed after the former Governor of New South Wales, Sir Thomas Brisbane. Although freemen were not allowed to settle within 50 miles of the colony, this ban was never really effective, and the penal function was in any case brought to an end in 1842. There was some economic competition for a while with the nearby port of Cleveland, but it ended in 1854 when the wharves of this town burned down! The way was now open for Brisbane to become the leading port.

Brisbane was one of the first really successful European settlements to be founded on the Australian continent. Men had gone to India to make their fortunes but had died by the score because of tropical diseases. But in Australia the virulent illnesses were not endemic and, despite the odd outbreak, the population remained healthy.

Many historic buildings survive from the early part of Brisbane's history. In 1829, Captain Patrick Logan built the Government Stores and Commissariat at the Moreton Bay Settlement. This building still stands where it was built, though the surroundings have changed so much that Captain Logan would probably not recognise his own work. It is now in the shadow of the riverside expressway. But perhaps the most historic of all Brisbane's old buildings is the Deanery of Saint John's Cathedral. In 1859, it was the venue for a momentous occasion; the proclaiming of the colony of Queensland from its balcony. From that moment on, all the land north of the Macpherson Range was free of control from Sydney. Though the Colony's finances got off to a fairly shaky start, it was not long before they began to improve. The vast inland grasslands became the home of thousands of sheep and cattle, while the sugar cane plantations prospered along the coast. The increasing wealth of the colony brought money and people to Brisbane, which grew from the humble penal settlement to become a bustling metropolis.

Given city status in 1902, Brisbane now covers an area of 970 square kilometres encircled by hills, and has a population of over one million people. To the north-west are the Glasshouse mountains formed from now extinct volcanoes; west are the rolling plains of the Darling Downs and to the south is the Lamington National Park, with the Gold Coast itself only 32 kilometres away. A famous attraction is the Lone Pine Koala Sanctuary where these cuddly creatures can be seen and photographed in their natural habitat.

A few degrees south of the Tropic of Capricorn, evergreen Brisbane has a year-round average of 7.5 hours of sunshine a day. The jacaranda and red bloomed poinciana trees add colour to the streets and in New Park Farm, on the banks of the river, twelve thousand rose bushes add their bouquet to the clear air. There is also the 20 hectare Botanic Gardens; Queen's Gardens; Victoria Park and, north of the city, Bunya Park Wildlife Sanctuary with its kangaroos, wallabies and koalas. The Mount Coot-tha Botanic Gardens have a Tropical Display Dome and the wonderful Sir Thomas Brisbane Planetarium.

There are so many things to see and do in sunny Brisbane...at Eagle Farm airport there is the 'Southern Cross', a Fokker tri-motor aircraft which was the first to cross the Pacific

Facing page Brisbane City Hall.
Overleaf Brisbane by night.

MLC

AMP

Ocean. This notable achievement was made by the famous Australian pilot Sir Charles Kingsford-Smith, who was born in Brisbane. Take a trip to Moreton, Stradbroke or Bribie Islands which offer fabulous surfing. Visit the Steam Locomotive Museum at Redbank or near Beenleigh there is Bullen's African Lion Safari. Overlooking the city is the Old Observatory on Wickham Terrace. Built by convicts in 1828 as a windmill, it never really worked properly, so they were made to crush grain by walking a treadmill! It has also seen service as a signal point, meteorological station and gallows. Newstead House overlooks the river at Breakfast Creek and was built in 1846 by Patrick Leslie, the first settler on the Darling Downs. It is the oldest home in the city and currently serves as the headquarters of the Royal Historical Society of Queensland. In George Street, within the Department of Aboriginal and Island Affairs, is a display of Aboriginal artifacts and crafts.

Then there are the beaches. The tropical weather around Brisbane is softened by the welcome, cooling sea breezes. Broad, white, sandy beaches stretch as far as the eye can see along the Sunshine Coast, north of Brisbane, and the Gold Coast, south of the city. Not only is the weather ideal for holidays, with a summer average of 25 degrees, but the waves are as well. Whether you like large rollers for surfing or gentle waves to swim in you can find them somewhere around Brisbane. One of the favourite resorts is on Bribie Island. Here beautiful beaches are backed by forests full of wonderful plant and animal life.

Why not try some of the seafood which makes Brisbane famous? You need not be a gourmet to enjoy Moreton Bay bugs, Queensland mudcrab, barramundi, reef fish, king or tiger prawn. You can even have a meal on the 'Captain Cook', a floating restaurant which operates from North Quay.

There is something for everyone in the rambling, sun-city of Brisbane: look through this wonderful new collection of colour photographs and meander through the city's streets and parks - the capital of sunshine and surf, gateway to the riches of Queensland.

Facing page Brisbane.
Overleaf Brisbane's Queen Street Mall.

HAUS BiLAS
SALE

ON THE MA

Above Brisbane and the Riverside Expressway seen from North Quay. Located on a bend in the Brisbane River Parliament Houses both old *right* and new, overshadow the Botanic Gardens *top*, which feature a superb display of tropical plants. *Facing page, top* Victoria Bridge and the city from the Cultural Centre. *Facing page, bottom* the William Jolly Bridge, which links South Brisbane with the central part of the city. *Overleaf* Brisbane's commercial area by night.

AMP
MLC
MLC
GWA
GWA

CityMutual
CityMutual
NATIONAL BANK
SOCIETE GENERALE
AMP

AMP
GWA

On October 27, 1728, in a small village in Yorkshire, England, the wife of a Scottish farm labourer gave birth to a son, and named him James. From this unlikely beginning the story of Queensland unfolds, for the child's full name was James Cook and he was destined to become a captain in His Britannic Majesty's Navy. For centuries philosophers had argued that there must be a great continent in the southern hemisphere to balance those in the north. Then, during the seventeenth and eighteenth centuries, Dutch and British captains brought back reports of strange and wild coasts far to the southeast of India. Was this the long sought *'Terra Australis'*?

By 1768, Cook's remarkable gifts of charting and surveying had brought him to the attention of their Lordships and he was put in command of *HMS Endeavour* on a quite remarkable expedition. After taking some scientists to Tahiti to view the transit of Venus, he was to sail on to find the Great Southern Continent. Striking across the trade routes, Cook found and charted two large islands, which later became known as New Zealand, before sailing on into unknown waters. Captain Cook then came across a coast running north-south; he decided to sail north. As he coasted peacefully northwards naming and charting bays that would one day be great cities, Captain Cook was sailing into deadly danger. The 'greatest navigator of history' had managed to sail into some of the most dangerous waters in the world. By keeping close to the coast he had slipped inside the Great Barrier Reef, which could easily rip the bottom out of the *Endeavour.*

Suddenly, in the middle of the night, the *Endeavour* struck the reef with a sickening crash. She was stuck fast. In a desperate attempt to clear the reef before the ship was broken up, stores were transferred to boats, or thrown overboard. Finally, they fought their way free of the reef and put ashore for repairs near present-day Cooktown. After navigating the whole of the east coast Captain Cook landed on Possession Island, off Cape York, and claimed the whole eastern half of the continent for King George III.

Though the first British settlements were far to the south, around Port Jackson, it was not long before explorers moved northwards. In 1821, the Surveyor-General of the colony of New South Wales, John Oxley, explored the area around Moreton Bay. As he gazed upon the rich land, Oxley decided it would be the ideal area for a settlement. Three years later he returned with convicts and troops to found a penal colony at Edenglassie. Then, with typical bureaucratic foresight, free farmers were banned from living within fifty miles of the site, effectively closing some 4,000 square miles of fertile land to settlement.

But no amount of government interference could keep down the adventurous spirit of the early Australians. In 1827, Alan Cunningham rode across the Darling Downs and came back with glowing reports of what he had found. Within a few years cattle, and their herders, had spread north to the Tropic of Capricorn and west towards the deserts. It was the vast open plains that were the first impetus to settlement in Queensland. Cattle ranching became big business as herds numbering in their thousands spread across the land.

With the cattle came sheep, unlike in the American West where cattlemen and sheepmen were continually at each others' throats. Indeed, the raising of sheep was rivalling that of cattle after just a few years. Almost all the wool produced was of the fine, merino variety, and it was produced in vast quantities. At Tinnenburra, south of Cunnamulla, could be found the largest woolshed in the world, there being a hundred sheepshearing stands. Through this town would tramp 'Scandalous Grahame', on his regular beat from Charleville to Bourke and back via Thargomindah. 'Scandalous Grahame' was the name of an itinerant worker who wandered the plains of Queensland in search of work. In his day he was the acknowledged champion yarn-spinner of the outback, telling amusing or terrifying stories so tall that people would hire him just to listen to his tales.

'Scandalous Grahame' belonged to an almost legendary breed; the swagmen. The tough, independent outlook of these wandering workers of the old Australian outback is perhaps best illustrated in a song; the famous *Waltzing Matilda.* The verses known to all Australians, and to most other people as well, were penned by one Banjo Patterson when he, too, was: "sat by a billabong, under the shade of a coolabah tree"

Previous pages Brisbane seen across Town Reach. *Facing page* a Barrier Reef island.

though whether he ever leapt into the water is open to question. The billabong in question is the Combo Billabong in central Queensland south of Kynuna. This water hole is on the Diamantina River which, on occasion, flows southwest into the Channel Country.

This vast area of land sprawls across the state, south of Mount Isa, and is characterised by vast plains cut by dry riverbeds, gullies and channels. Though there is very little rainfall, the grasslands get an annual dousing of water. Following the 'Big Wet' to the north and east, the Georgina and Diamantina Rivers, together with Cooper Creek, become raging torrents, bringing life-giving moisture to the plains. Lush growths of grass, wild flowers and plants spring up from the virtual desert, and the cattle are moved in by the drovers for fattening. But the terrible heat and bone-dry ground take their toll of the rivers. As they flow southwest, the streams and rivers get smaller and slower, until they disappear entirely; it is a very rare year that the waters of the 'Big Wet' actually reach Lake Eyre. This gradual evaporation is best shown near Windorah, a town fabled far and wide for the excellence of its pub. Northeast of the town is the only place in the world where two rivers, the Barcoo and the Thomson, join to form a creek, the Cooper.

It was across the Channel Country that Captain Starlight drove his stolen cattle to market. Having rustled the cattle on the grasslands around Longreach, he rebranded them and herded them across the Channel Country to Birdsville. From there he took them south along the Birdsville Track, which he had helped to pioneer, to the railhead at Marree and eventual sale in the markets of South Australia.

In the heart of the Channel Country, just northwest of Lake Yamma Yamma, stands a triangular willow post. On two sides of the post are inscribed 'Queensland' and the third 'South Australia'. This is the famous Haddon Corner where the boundary between the two colonies was first set and marked over a hundred years ago. Indeed, the climate is so dry and predictable that the post has survived since 1880.

Lake Yamma Yamma, itself, is another wonder of the outback. Along with most of the other lakes of the interior, Yamma Yamma is usually bone dry, only filling every forty years or so. But when the lake has water, it displays a remarkable characteristic. The shores of Yamma Yamma are so flat and level that a steady wind can literally move the waters of the lake several kilometres in any direction.

On an evening in 1923, John Campbell Miles, who is otherwise unknown to history, camped by the banks of the Leichardt River and made a discovery that would change the history of the area. He found a magnificent lode of silver-lead ore, and is now credited with founding the city of Mount Isa itself. Naming the place Mount Isabelle, after his sister, John Miles later saw the fields taken over by the giant Mount Isa Mines Limited. This company is now the driving force behind the economic life of the city and has financed many exploration projects which have resulted in copper being added to the list of ores in the area. The total ore reserves are currently estimated at some 100 million tonnes.

The city, whose inhabitants number around thirty thousand, has always been careful to secure its future. Over the years the city authorities have extended their boundaries to ensure that no new finds of ore will be outside their jurisdiction. This policy has led to the city of Mount Isa now extending over more land than the Kingdom of the Netherlands. Lying at the heart of the arid grasslands of Queensland, Mount Isa was always short of water, the flow of the Leichardt River being only seasonal. In 1958, however, the river was dammed to form Lake Moondarra a few miles north of the town. This has become not only a secure source of water but also a favourite leisure area. People flock to the lake for swimming, boating and most other water sports. But one of the most critical problems facing the first miners was how to get their precious metals to market. Brisbane was an impossible 1,400 kilometres away while the much nearer coast of the Gulf of Carpentaria was a mass of mangrove swamp and inhospitable shore. The answer was to build a great railway, whose line is now followed by the Flinders Highway, to a small, sugar-exporting port by the name of Townsville.

The Leichardt river perpetuates the name of one of early Australia's great pioneers. Ludwig

Facing page and overleaf the Gold Coast.

CHATEAU

ALLUNGA

TEN
BAR & RESTAURANT
PARADISE CENTRE

Leichardt came to Australia from his native Germany in the first half of the nineteenth century and was soon involved in charting the interior. In 1844, he set off from Moreton Bay heading for the coast of the Northern Territory. The epic journey across the unknown to Port Essington took many months and carried him across the river that still bears his name. In 1848, he set out on an even more ambitious journey to cross the continent from east to west, and was never seen again.

Leichardt was not the only explorer of the region who met a tragic end. Eighteen years after Leichardt's death, his path was crossed by four intrepid men on their way from Melbourne to the Gulf of Carpentaria. Burke and Wills were leading an expedition, sponsored by the Royal Society of Victoria, with the aim of crossing the continent from south to north. The expedition had begun with nearly fifty camels and horses and plenty of supplies, but at Cooper Creek this small advance party had pushed on alone. The party reached the tidal swamps of northern Queensland, but on the return journey they missed the rearguard by just nine and a half hours, and were left alone in the centre of the Channel Country. By the time anyone found them, three of the four were dead.

Ironically, while these explorers of the hinterland were dying of thirst, they were sitting on top of one of the largest natural reserves of fresh water in the world. The Great Artesian Basin stretches under 1,760,000 square kilometres of the outback. Water that falls as rain far from the hot deserts of the interior seeps through layers of porous rock until it lies as a vast reservoir, deep below the surface of the land. Bore holes drilled down from the surface can tap this great water supply and make arid areas capable of supporting life. It has been estimated that some 20 per cent of Australia's sheep, including those of the Channel Country, are dependent on artesian water for at least part of the year.

But the water of the Artesian Basin and the silver, lead and copper of Mount Isa are not the only natural resources to lie buried beneath the parched soil of the Queensland outback. In 1872 on the Listowel Downs, not far from the beat of 'Scandalous Grahame', opals were found. Other opal strikes followed at Kyabra and Yowah while sapphires and rubies turned up west of Rockhampton. The area around Anakie blossomed with gem boom towns to which the miners gave such imaginative names as Sapphire, Rubyvale and Emerald. It was at one of these settlements that the 'Star of Queensland' was found. At the time, however, the lucky finder did not realise what the dirty, misshapen stone was, and so used it as a doorstop. Eventually, somebody recognised the sapphire for what it was and it was sent to America for cutting. The resulting 'star' is said to be worth hundreds of thousands of dollars.

To the southeast of the gem fields, indeed to the southeast of almost everything in Queensland, is Brisbane, the state capital. This is the city that grew from John Oxley's convict settlement of Edenglassie. The policy of banning free settlement officially ended in 1842, though it had been flouted for years, and the city began to compete in importance with the nearby port of Cleveland. In 1854, the wharves and port facilities of Cleveland tragically burnt down and the town retired into graceful obscurity. This left Brisbane free to grow and prosper, so that when Queensland became a colony in 1859, the treasury held a full 7½d.

Though Brisbane was not given city status until 1902, it now covers an area of 970 square kilometres and has a population of over one million people. The city is placed in a magnificent natural setting on the Brisbane River. To the northwest are the Glasshouse mountains formed from old, extinct volcanoes; west are the rolling plains of the Darling Downs and to the south is the Lamington National Park, with the Gold Coast itself only 32 kilometres away. A famous attraction is the Lone Pine Koala Sanctuary, where these cuddly creatures can be seen and photographed in their natural habitat.

A few degrees south of the Tropic of Capricorn, evergreen Brisbane has a year-round average of over seven hours of sunshine a day. The jacaranda and red-bloomed poinciana trees add colour to the streets and in New Park Farm, on the banks of the river, twelve thousand rose bushes add their bouquet to the clear air. There is also the 20 hectare Botanic Gardens; Queen's Gardens; Victoria Park and, north of the city, Bunya Park Wildlife Sanctuary with its kangaroos, wallabies and koalas. In the Mount Coot-tha Botanic Gardens is the Tropical Display Dome and the wonderful Sir Thomas Brisbane Planetarium.

Facing page Surfers Paradise. *Overleaf* the Gold Coast.

SURF LIFE SAVING
ASSOCIATION
4GG
VH-SUF
RESCUE
Westpac Banking Corporation

THE MARK
GOLDEN ORCHID
The Sands
MONTE CARLO
SAHARA COURT
JOLIMONT

But it is not only for tropical splendour that visitors come to the city of Brisbane; they also come for the food. The rich, blue waters of the rolling Pacific yield a bountiful harvest of some of the most delicious seafood known to man. Moreton Bay bugs, Queensland mudcrab, barramundi, reef fish, king and tiger prawn share the menu with tuna, marlin and mackerel at the best tables in Brisbane.

But the really booming industry in eastern Queensland is not to be found in the industrial hub of Brisbane. The big business of tourism is making the coasts to the north and south of the capital wealthier than ever before. The wonderful combination of broad, sandy beaches and a relaxing tropical climate have made the Gold Coast and the Sunshine Coast the holiday resorts of Australia. Families flock to the coast from the interior to soak up the sun and the sea. At such towns as Surfers Paradise and Maroochydore the beaches are thronged with surfers and swimmers, each intent on making a splash with any of the watching 'sheilas'.

But the State of Queensland does not stop at the coast. Off the shore runs one of the great wonders of the natural world. The Great Barrier Reef is now the adventure playground of any who care to take advantage of the beautiful islands and glorious climate so many kilometres out to sea. Much of the economy of northern Queensland rests on the hordes of visitors that pour into the area. But for many years the reef was nothing but a danger to shipping and an inhibition to the prosperity of the coastal regions it skirted.

The Great Barrier Reef is one of the world's great wonders: the most massive structure built by any living organism. It stretches for 2,012 kilometres, from Gladstone to Cape York, covering 207,200 square kilometres and may rise to 200 feet from the ocean floor. The distance from the outer reef to the continental mainland varies from 25 kilometres in the north to 400 kilometres in the south. On the leeward side near the coast are over 700 tropical islands which chequer the dazzling sea.

In fact composed of thousands of separate banks, the mighty reef took many millions of years to form. The tiny, soft-bodied animals, known as coral polyps, which built the reef, like to live in tropical waters where the surf crashes. To protect themselves from the foaming waters, these small creatures deposit small limestone tubes in which they live. Over the centuries, as generation after generation of polyp live and die, the concretion of limestone is built up, and it is this that forms the reefs. There are at least 350 species of coral present, growing in their millions in different forms and colours, forming a kaleidoscope within a sun-drenched sea.

The marine life is unsurpassed. Well known to big-game fishermen are the black marlin, swordfish and barracuda. But there are shoals of other brightly-hued fish. This is home for the wrasse, red emperors, parrot fish, angel fish, sweetlip, coral trout, demoiselles, the huge groper and the deadly, envenomed stonefish. There are lobsters, crabs, crayfish and prawns, colourful starfish, sea urchins, and the famous giant clams which grow to four feet across and weigh up to 200 pounds. Danger lurks in the water with jellyfish known as sea wasps, while on the beaches female green turtles haul themselves above the high-tide mark to lay and hide their eggs before sunrise marks them for the predator. The reef is an excellent breeding ground for birds. You may see the white-breasted sea eagle, or an osprey wheeling in the warm air. Down below, soft coral waves in the ocean current alongside other family members: brain corals, staghorns, organ pipes, mushroom corals and blue coral. This is nature at its most abundant, aided by warm waters which only range seasonally between 21 and 38 degrees centigrade.

Whether by land or water Queensland is a fascinating place. The moving waters of Lake Yamma Yamma and the incessantly crashing surf of the Great Barrier Reef can be joined by a line spanning the whole breadth of the state. Across this line have wandered Captain Starlight, 'Scandalous Grahame' and gem miners; together they have written the story of Queensland – a story of drama and legend which will continue into the future.

Facing page, top Surfers Paradise.
Facing page, bottom Southport.

The Gold Coast, south of Brisbane, is one of the premier holiday resorts of Queensland. The relaxed, carefree feeling of a Surfers Paradise shopping centre *these pages*, with its colourful streetside restaurants and giant chess set *left*, reflects well the Gold Coast's infectious and all-pervasive holiday atmosphere.

Coke
Coca-Cola

CINZANO
VERMOUTH
PIE SHOP

Southern Queensland's natural splendours: Cedar Creek *facing page;* Curtis Falls *left;* the commanding view from Tamborine Mountain *top. Above* abseilers pause for lunch by Ballanjui Falls.

Left and top the Sunshine Pineapple Plantation. *Above* the home of Andrew Fisher, the first Queenslander to become Prime Minister, in Gympie. *Facing page: top left and bottom left* the Jondaryan Woolshed Museum, *centre* Gympie and *bottom right* a local museum, *top right* a hotel in Wooroolin.

Catching pens - 2 shearers catch from each pen. Each shearer has own letting out gate with holding pen outside.

XXXX
GRAND HOTEL

IMPERIAL HOTEL
XXXX The popular beer
Bewick Bishop & Connolly
Fair Foul

Left the 'Singing Ship' memorial to the famed navigator Captain Cook, at Emu Park, near the popular coastal resort of Yeppoon. *Top* the Heritage Tavern is a magnificent example of Rockhampton's architectural charm. *Above* the Queensland National Hotel in the mining town of Mount Morgan. *Facing page: top* boom netting off Great Keppel Island *bottom right. Bottom left* Rosslyn Harbour, near Yeppoon.

Right and below right 'road train' cattle transporter and stock at Springsure, 600 kilometres northwest of Brisbane. *Below and bottom left* cotton plants and ginnery at Emerald, the main town in the western Capricornia region. *Bottom right* another facet of Queensland's mixed economy;

the Blair Athol open-cast coal pit at Clermont, north of Springsure. *Facing page* fossicking for gemstones is a popular pastime with visitors, as well as a way of life for miners around the town of Rubyville, near Emerald. A $5 'Miner's Right' entitles anyone to chance their hand at striking it rich.

The peaceful and historic city of Charters Towers *this page*, inland of Townsville, is one of Queensland's gold rush towns. In its heyday it housed over 30,000 souls. Today, the town relies mainly on cattle, together with citrus fruit and grape growing, for its income, although many reminders of its former wealth and glory remain. *Top right* Stock Exchange Arcade and City Hall. *Top left* the Australian Bank of Commerce. *Centre* Gill Street. *Left* interior of the Stock Exchange Arcade. *Facing page* situated 70 kilometres east of Charters Towers via Mingella lies the gold-mining 'ghost town' of Ravenswood, where derelict wooden buildings and discarded, rusting machinery serve to create a poignant and lasting reminder of the town's active past. *Top* the Railway Hotel. *Bottom* the Imperial Hotel.

IMPERIAL
HOTEL

Historically, sheep and cattle have always been the mainstays of Queensland's economy and whilst mining, tourism and manufacture have become increasingly important wealth producers, it is the huge areas of grassland that are still of paramount importance. In recent years, however, considerable improvements have been made to the per-acre yield of both beef and wool. The photographs *these pages* illustrate the seemingly timeless scenes of outdoor life at Silver Hills Inland Resort.

Coca Coala

The Mount Isa Rodeo *these pages*, held in August of each year, is perhaps the most important annual social and sporting event in the city's calendar, visitors virtually doubling the population. Townsville *overleaf* is a major Queensland port, handling the minerals from the Mount Isa mines.

JRC

4AY
RADIO
4AY
HAYLES

These pages colourful denizens of the Great Barrier Reef. Sea cucumbers *this page* are to be found in all the world's oceans but nowhere else do they exhibit such a fantastic variety of form and colour. These slug-like creatures can grow up to 2 metres in length. Even the worms *facing page,* such as the giant tube worm *bottom left,* the blue flat worm *bottom right* and the flat worm *top* appear excitingly attractive in Queensland's coastal waters.

Previous pages Heron Island on the Great Barrier Reef. *These pages* some of the colourful fish that live on the reef. *Above* the Beaked Coralfish. The Zebra Lionfish *facing page, bottom* seems to openly invite attack by displaying it 'plumage' – poisonous spines are its protection.

The ragged-finned Turkey Fish *below right* is a member of the scorpion fish family that also possesses a venomous defence mechanism. *Above right* a common Cleaner Wrasse removes parasites from the gills of a larger fish. *Facing page, top* Coral Cod. *Below* Many-lined Sweetlips.

Seen from the air, the Cairns region of Queensland *these pages* is a land of lush, tropical vegetation and magnificent beaches washed by a turquoise sea. These warm, reef-protected waters are home to a host of fascinating creatures, including the superb marlin fish that attracts big-game fishermen to the area. Cairns is the gateway to the tropical north and serves as a stepping-off point for the Great Barrier Reef as well as for some of Queensland's most enticing islands.

The Atherton Tableland is a scenic plateau that consists of both dense rainforests and graceful waterfalls such as those pictured at Malanda *above* and Millaa Millaa *top*. *Right* the Kuranda Railway Viaduct. *Facing page* is shown the amazing curtain fig tree near the tourist town of Tinaburra.

CURTAIN FIG TREE Ficus virens

These pages less commercialised than the beaches of the Gold and Sunshine Coasts of Queensland, those that are situated around Port Douglas *above, right and facing page, top* and Cairns *top and facing page, bottom,* in the north of the state, are among the best in the world.

Sugar *top and facing page, top,* bananas *right and above* and more recently tea, as at the automated and mechanised Narinda

Plantation *facing page, bottom* are all major crops in the agricultural region around Cairns, at the base of the Cape York Peninsula.

Cairns *these pages and overleaf*, 'capital' of tropical Queensland, is an important commercial centre and the state's most northerly city. Originally founded by disgruntled miners in 1876, to service the goldfields of the north, Cairns soon became the elegant and prosperous hub of an area given over to sugar cane production. Sugar remains an important local commodity, with the Cairns bulk sugar terminal handling much of the region's output.

Faux Pas
HAPPY DAZE
CAIRNS

The native Australian's world-renowned passion for water sports is amply demonstrated at Cairns Marina *these pages.* *Overleaf* Cairns.

328116

Sydney bursts upon the visitor in an array of unexpected colour and vitality. Most people know of the Opera House and the Harbour Bridge, but very few are prepared for the majesty of their setting. Resplendent against the azure blue of the harbour or the twinkling city lights, they take on a totally unexpected beauty and elegance. The city itself is throbbing with life. The broad shopping streets of the city centre and the rich variety of cultures and influences are unmatched anywhere else in Australia. Indeed, Sydney is the only truly cosmopolitan city on the continent, having established trade links with China, America and Britain in its very earliest days, and is the the first port of call for most visitors to this wonderful country.

Sydneysiders, as they call themselves, know well how to enjoy their city. They are a remarkable people, being hardy, sophisticated, but above all, easy-going and relaxed in their attitudes. The sub-tropical climate of their city is an open invitation to those who enjoy outdoor sports, and that includes almost everyone in Sydney. There are tennis-courts, numerous parks and, perhaps most important of all, beaches. The typical Australian, and Sydneysiders are no exception, have fallen in love with beach life; indeed their whole culture may appear to be influenced by it. Long hours spent on the beach, soaking up the sunshine and watching the beautiful 'Sheilas' go by, interspersed with bursts of activity surfing or swimming is an integral part of the Sydneysider's life style. For those more interested in culture there are numerous concerts and plays put on throughout the city and, of course, there is the Opera House. Overlooking the Harbour, the graceful sweep of the Opera House's roof covers performances of the world's greatest operas, staged in lavish style as befits such a masterpiece of architecture.

This great city began life almost by accident. In 1770, after a long and arduous voyage, Captain Cook came across the long sought *Terra Australis Incognita.* Sailing north along the coast, he discovered and named many important coastal features. Among them was a large bay where he and his crew were astounded by the variety and beauty of the plant life. He named it Botany Bay. After sailing along the entire eastern coast of the continent, Cook returned home with his report on the new land. These reports were so impressive that the government decided to act upon them.

Consequently, eighteen years later, Captain Arthur Phillip was sent off with a fleet of ships, convicts, marines and orders to found a penal colony at Botany Bay. However, when Captain Phillip reached the proposed site of the new colony he found that it was entirely unsuitable; the land was unproductive and the bay could not protect his ships. So Captain Phillip decided to move the colony to another location, but first he had to find somewhere. One of the places that he explored was a bay that Captain Cook had named Port Jackson. Captain Phillip described it as "the finest harbour in the world, in which a thousand sail of the line may ride in the most perfect security." He set up his settlement on the shores of a small inlet, which he called Sydney Cove and which remains the main terminal for passenger liners to this day.

It was not long before people began to pour into the new settlement. First came convicts and then free settlers, trying to clear farms and make a livelihood from the untamed soil. The harsh days of early Sydney are recreated a short drive away, to the north of the modern city. Old Sydney Town stands on the Pacific Highway, near Gosford. Here cottages, convict huts, workshops and a replica ship have been constructed to recreate the look and atmosphere of the first European settlement on the continent. The town has been fully staffed with soldiers, convicts and craftsmen who act the parts of the original inhabitants.

By 1821, under the leadership of Governer Macquarie, Sydney had become bustling and respectable with hospitals, churches, schools and parks scattered throughout the town. The harsh days of the convict transportations were soon left far behind as Sydney grew

Facing page, top Macquarie Street, Sydney.
Facing page, bottom Kings Cross, Sydney. *Overleaf* the Opera House.

AMP

QANTAS
IBM

to be the most important financial centre and largest city on the continent: by 1900 almost half a million people lived in Sydney. For a few years Sydney was overtaken in importance by Melbourne, but today it has reassumed its place as the first city in Australia.

The city of Sydney, in the closing years of this century, extends across 700 square miles of New South Wales and has a population in excess of three million. The tremendous area is due to the desire of every Australian to own his own home. Throughout the suburbs, Sydney is a city of wide streets and low bungalows. It is only in the heart of the city that tall skyscrapers rise and even here imaginative architecture and a sensible approach have created an appealing and cohesive whole, reflecting the city's dynamism and energy.

The undisputed playground of Sydney is the suburb of Manly. The beaches and facilities here are hard to match, while the climate is ideal. The cove earned its name in the time of Captain Phillip. He was impressed by the proud bearing of the local Aborigines and so named the area Manly. The bathing and surfing is so much a part of the suburb that it is strange to think that there was once a time when such activities were illegal. In 1838 a law was passed which banned public bathing between 6 am and 8 pm. By 1902, it was clear that Manly's major asset was being ruined by this law and a local newspaperman decided to force the issue. Mr. W H Gocher announced that he would bathe in public every day, and nobody arrested him. From that time on the beaches of Manly became increasingly popular, establishing a tradition that is truly Australian. Another great invention came to the area with a gardener called Tommy Tanner, who hailed from the South Sea Islands. Much to the surprise of the locals Tommy would throw himself into the largest waves and ride them to the shore. It wasn't long before someone thought of doing it on a plank of wood, and surfing was born.

Commercial hub of the South Pacific, Sydney is a capital city in all but name – it is the cultural and industrial centre of a rapidly expanding nation.

Facing page, top and bottom Sydney Harbour.

CANBERRA

ROYAL VIKING STAR
SYDNEY HARBOUR EXPLORER

BARCLAYS
NORWICH
CITICORP
MENZIES HOTEL
Travelodge

Previous pages a magnificent aerial view of the Sydney city centre. Chinatown *these pages* is a noted nightspot with its collection of restaurants and bars. *Overleaf* the many faces of Sydney Harbour.

AYSUN
LICENSED
Restaurant
DIXON
SNACK BAR

Previous pages Sydney and Port Jackson from the west. *Left, top and facing page, bottom* the Harbour Bridge.

Other landmarks of Sydney are: *above* the El Alamein Fountain and *facing page, top* the restored Pier One.

Legal & General

Previous pages the city from Victoria Road at Wrights Point. Narrabeen *above* lies to the north of Sydney. Manly Beach *top, right, facing page, top and facing page, bottom* is one of the finest and most popular of Sydney's surfing grounds. The beach was given its name by Captain Phillip in 1788 because he was so impressed by the masculinity of the local Aborigines. *Overleaf* can be seen Bondi Beach, perhaps the most famous of all Australian beaches.

New South Wales is the oldest and most important state in Australia. Stretching across more than a tenth of the continent, New South Wales is centred on Sydney, a city of some three million inhabitants. Famous throughout the world for its high quality wool, the state has far more to offer, however, than a lot of sheep! The Hunter Valley produces Australia's finest wines which, together with the excellent cuisine, make dining in New South Wales one of the great joys of life in Australia. The whole state is imbued with history; be it the stolid, persevering farmers who made New South Wales the way it is, or the wild and exciting bushrangers, such as Ned Kelly and Captain Thunderbolt, who added an important chapter to the legends of the past.

Though it wasn't until 1788 that colonisation began in New South Wales, men had been determined to visit the area for hundreds of years. In ancient times, the possible existence of a large continent far to the south of the civilised world, a *Terra Australis Incognita,* was the subject of hot debate. After all, it was reasoned, the globe needed a large southern landmass to balance that in the north. In 480 B.C. the Carthaginians sent out a fleet to settle the question once and for all, but all they managed to prove was the fact that Africa is very big indeed. A slightly better attempt was made by the Spaniard, Pedro Fernández de Quirós, in 1605. Using the same reasoning as the Carthaginians had two thousand years earlier, de Quirós sailed from Peru convinced that the inhabitants of the *Terra Australis* were just waiting for him to arrive so that they could all become good Catholics. After many days of hard sailing he landed on the New Hebrides, proudly announced that he had discovered 'Austrialia', claimed it for Spain and sailed away again. His subordinate, Luis de Torres, then went on to reach the East Indies, sailing through the straits that bear his name and, by an amazing feat of seamanship, managing to miss Australia altogether.

Despite these attempts to find the great southern continent, its actual discovery was left to a Dutchman who was trying to find New Guinea. When Willem Jansz sighted part of the Cape York Peninsula he didn't realise quite what he had found. Luckily a lot of other people did. By the end of the century a succession of Dutch explorers had formed a pretty good idea of what the southern landmass was like. As Dutch interest waned, so British interest grew. In 1768, Captain James Cook left Britain to chart the coast of what was now called *Terra Australis* or 'New Holland' depending on whether or not you were Dutch.

On April 20, 1770, the coast of southeastern Australia was finally sighted and the charting could begin. As Captain Cook sailed up the eastern coast he landed several times, on one occasion exploring and naming Botany Bay, before reaching Possession Island. Here, on August 23, he named the whole of eastern Australia 'New South Wales' and claimed it for King George III. The reports that Captain Cook brought back on this, and subsequent voyages, indicated that Australia was a land of wealth and opportunity, thus establishing a reputation that the land has kept for over two hundred years.

Cook's glowing reports, plus the fact that America had just become unavailable due to a short war, decided the British government on a course of action; they would send 730 convicts to New South Wales. In charge of the expedition was Arthur Phillip and he had about 200 marines to keep order. Phillip soon realised that Botany Bay was not a good place to start a colony so he moved everyone a few miles north to Port Jackson. Here Sydney Cove was named and settled and the business of government began on February 7, 1788.

Over the next few years the settlement at Sydney prospered and grew steadily. The system by which convicts worked on farms until their sentence was up, when they could gain a farm of their own, worked quite well for some years. Farmers and pastoralists pushed out from Sydney into the hinterland until the 'nineteen counties' had been established. In time, decent men of good reputation were induced to sail to New South Wales by government promises of free land, free labour and guaranteed markets for their products. Sheep rearing became increasingly important in the economy of the colony as the area of settled land grew steadily, despite the protests of the local Aborigines. With the expansion of agriculture and grazing into the interior, Sydney's importance as a port advanced enormously. As the population and wealth of the town grew, the opportunity for small scale industry and commercial activity appeared. This added to the population and prosperity of the town, creating a spiral of wealth.

Facing page, top Bach Beach, near Coffs Harbour. *bottom* Coffs Harbour Beach.

By the second decade of the nineteenth century, Governor Macquarie felt that the colony was rich enough to merit some public buildings. He therefore engaged Francis Greenway, who had been transported for forgery, to design several buildings in the fashionable Regency style; perhaps the most famous of these is St James' Church which is still extant. Greenway was not the only convict to find importance in Macquarie's administration, the governor taking the view that ex-convicts should be given positions of trust and responsibility as part of their rehabilitation. In 1821 Macquarie was recalled to London.

Despite Governor Macquarie's optimism, the economy of the colony did not really boom until the 1850s. As with many new colonies the wealth of agriculture was enough to keep things ticking over, but it was mineral wealth which made New South Wales more than just an Imperial offshoot. The discoveries of gold in the 1850s and 60s gave the great impetus to growth in the colony; migrants flowed in creating a great demand for consumer and manufactured goods. In the following thirty years the population of Sydney grew from 60,000 to 400,000, and the rest of the state followed suit.

In the great mining towns that grew up around the gold, and later silver, deposits the authorities were sometimes hard pressed to maintain law and order. They found it particularly difficult to make the stubborn, independent 'Diggers' pay their taxes; the miners, like a lot of other people, failing to appreciate the government's right to their hard-earned gold. The situation came to a head in the summer of 1854 at Ballarat in Victoria. Following the suspected murder of a miner by the authorities, the diggers organised themselves into military companies and began work on a stockade which they called Eureka. Faced with open rebellion, the governor of Victoria acted swiftly and, on December 3, troops arrived at the Eureka Stockade. The 150 diggers inside the stockade bravely defied the troops, and the rebellion which has become the rallying cry for present-day republicanism began. Fifteen minutes later the rebellion was over and peace returned to the goldfields. The episode at Ballarat did, however, worry the Imperial administration, with the result that important reforms were soon introduced.

Another popular manifestation of contempt for authority was the era of the bushranger, the last and most famous of whom was Ned Kelly. Born Edward Kelly in 1855, he took to the bush in 1877 with the police hot on his trail after a horse-stealing incident. He joined with his brother, Dan, who was also on the run and for three years the Kelly Gang, which had several members, pulled off a variety of daring robberies. But the best-known part of the Ned Kelly story is the innovation of bulletproof armour, which was worn by every member of the gang. The construction of this armour is held up as both example and proof of the intelligence and thoroughness of the most famous gang of all. Despite this protection a vicious fight, at Glenrowan in 1880, ended when the whole gang was shot dead by police, except Ned himself, who was badly wounded. A few months later Ned Kelly was hanged at Melbourne and the era of the bushranger came to an end. In their time, and increasingly since, the activities of such men as Ned Kelly have become romanticised and the bushranger has become the hero of the people for his attacks on the wealthy squatters.

But no matter how romantic and adventurous the bushrangers, they played only a small part in the development of the colony. It was the steady, repetitive work of the farmers and miners that built the foundations on which modern New South Wales is built. In 1883, a German migrant, by the name of Charles Rasp, who had come to the new land in search of fame and fortune, was travelling through the outback some 700 kilometres west of Tooraweenah. Here, on the slopes of Broken Hill, he found one of the world's most astounding deposits of silver and lead. Resisting the urge to dash to the nearest town to announce his good fortune, which would inevitably have meant that everybody except Charles Rasp would have become rich, he headed back towards civilisation. By 1885, Rasp had founded the Broken Hill Proprietary Company and mining operations could get underway. Three years later Broken Hill became a town and, in 1907, a city. As the town grew, so did Charles Rasp's company until it became the largest private industrial company in Australia. To this day Broken Hill continues to produce some 2 million tonnes of ore per year, though ironically the Broken Hill Proprietary Company no longer owns any of the mines there.

Facing page, top banana plantation near Grafton. *bottom* Moonee Beach near Coffs Harbour.

New South Wales is, of course, well-known for its sheep. Seventy million of them roam the grasslands of the hinterland, together with some five million cattle. The fine Merino sheep, which are the most common breed, are said to have been first brought to Australia, by somewhat underhand means, for the quality of their wool. The pastoral land on which the grazing farms depend is concentrated on the wide, western slopes of the Great Dividing Range. From the earliest days of Sydney, settlers had been trying to find a way over the mountains, if for no other reason than to see what was there. In 1813, W.C. Wentworth managed to cross the mountains, to be followed two years later by the surveyor G.W. Evans, who reported on the rich, broad grazing land to be found. That was enough for the settlers, who poured over the mountains with their herds until the region was the most productive grazing country on the continent.

In the far west is a vast area of near desert, which is perhaps the most fascinating area of the whole state. Stretching north from the Darling River are great areas of arid grassland on which graze some two million sheep, which produce about 60,000 bales of wool per year. This land is also grazed by the ubiquitous kangaroo, now staging a comeback in terms of numbers. In the extreme northwest of the area is Sturt National Park, covering an area of almost 200,000 hectares. Though the park is almost desert land, with little moisture and incredible heat, it is an important wildlife reserve. The kangaroos are joined here by large numbers of emus and wallabies and the area continually echoes to the calls and screeches of thousands of birds, which can be just as unpleasant for the visitor as the heat. Tourists might enjoy themselves more among the modern conveniences of White Cliffs, where there is the added bonus of, perhaps, finding a priceless opal.

The lifeblood of New South Wales is the Murray-Murrumbidgee-Darling river system. The waters that these rivers drain down from the Great Dividing Range bring life to vast areas of the state which would otherwise be desert. Today, large irrigation schemes throughout the river basins have greatly increased the productivity of the soil, and it is not only sheep and cattle that are raised here. The Murray River Valley is famous for its vineyards. Many of the grapes are dried on great trays in the sun to produce raisins or sultanas, but an increasing number of grapes are being fermented into wine. A use which, some would argue, is far more sensible. And the river is not only useful as a supply of water. Like the Mississippi in North America, the river system was an important transport link for the early settlers. The government recognised the importance of opening up a navigable river link and so a prize of £2,000 was offered for the first steamship to reach Swan Hill. Consequently, two ships, the *Lady Augusta* and the *Mary Ann*, the latter owned by one William Randell, lined up at the mouth of the Murray to race upstream. After a hard fought race, the *Mary Ann* steamed into Swan Hill way in the lead. But when William Randell went to collect the prize the bureaucrats told him that he couldn't have the money because his steamship did not fulfil the government's definition of a steamship. Needless to say, Mr Randell was not amused.

However, despite government quibbles, the river route had been opened up and for many years it was the main transport artery of the area. By the 1870s, there were over a hundred steamers plying the river, together with hundreds more barges. The large, sedate paddle steamers gently nosed their way up and down the waterways bringing supplies and news to the remote settlements along the riverbanks. It was at one of these out-of-the-way places, near Walwa, that a grey calf was born in 1907. Apart from the farmer on whose land it appeared, nobody was particularly startled by the news, mainly due to the fact that they didn't know about it. But within thirty years every Australian farmer worth his salt had heard of the Murray Grey. By the outbreak of the Second World War, the Grey had become a recognised breed and today it has become established in many parts of the continent, and indeed overseas.

The coastal regions of New South Wales remain the most populous area of the state. Historically, the coastal regions to the east of the Great Dividing Range were the easiest, and so the first, to be settled. As well as the rich agricultural land fringing the mountains there are many holiday resorts whose popularity increases by leaps and bounds every year. The villages and towns along the coast retain a rural atmosphere which makes for some of the most relaxed holidays in the world. Further north, around Sydney, the pace quickens as

Facing page, top and bottom Coffs Harbour.

LFB 6388

Wanderlust

surfing beaches and yacht harbours crowd in upon one another in a contest to gain the most visitors. Finally, the undisputed leader of surfing beaches is reached: Bondi. Here golden-tanned Adonis-like bodies cavort on surfboards amid the giant rollers in the hope of attracting the eyes of an admiring 'Sheila'. Even further towards the equator can be found the rainforests and deep gorges of the northern coastlands.

But the greatest city of New South Wales is still Sydney. The city founded so many years ago by Arthur Phillip has grown to become the most cultured and business-like city on the continent. It has become the communications hub for the whole state and, to some extent, of the whole continent. Road, rail and air networks are centred on the city and, more often than not, it is the first port of call for visitors to the country.

These visitors come expecting to see the Opera House and the Harbour Bridge, but they can hardly be prepared for the beautiful setting of the city. It is clear that Governor Phillip must have had more in mind than simple practicalities when he chose the site. Even today, with the proliferation of high-rise concrete buildings, the beauty of the Port Jackson area is clear to all.

Quite apart from the glories of its setting, the city is one of elegance and variety. The great shopping streets and civic architecture, some of it remaining from the days of Governor Macquarie, add an indefinable 'something' to Sydney that marks it out from all other cities of the continent. It is one of the most cosmopolitan cities in the world. Early links with Californian and Asian trades ensured that Sydney would always be more than just a small part of Britain. It created its own atmosphere and ambience which has persisted to the present day.

The Sydneysiders, as they call themselves, know well how to enjoy their wonderful city. The beautiful climate is an open invitation to anyone who enjoys outdoor sports; which means everyone. There are tennis courts, numerous parks and, perhaps most important of all, beaches. The typical Australian, and Sydneysiders are no exception, has fallen in love with beach life. Indeed it has been said, with some justification, that their whole culture has been based upon it. Long hours spent on the beach, soaking up the sunshine, interspersed with bursts of activity, surfing or swimming, is an integral part of the Sydneysider's character. For those more interested in culture, there are numerous concerts and plays put on throughout the city and, of course, there is the Opera House. Overlooking the Harbour, the graceful sweep of the Opera House's roof covers performances of the world's greatest operas, staged in lavish style as befits such a masterpiece of architecture.

The city of Sydney, in the closing years of this century, extends across 700 square miles of New South Wales and has a population in excess of three million. The tremendous area is due to the desire of every Australian to own his own home. Throughout the suburbs, Sydney is a city of wide streets and low bungalows. It is only in the heart of the city that tall skyscrapers rise and even here imaginative architecture and a sensible approach have created an appealing and cohesive whole, reflecting Sydney's dynamism and energy.

But the Sydneysiders have not forgotten the past in the rush for the future. A few kilometres to the north can be found Old Sydney Town, a replica of the early settlement in Sydney Cove. Here can be seen convict huts, shops and a period sailing ship; even the people are dressed as the original settlers. There are soldiers of the New South Wales Corps, magistrates and, of course, convicts. The town aims to be realistic in every way; if a convict misbehaves he is still dragged to the Market Place, tied to a post and horsewhipped into submission. The staff, however, make sure that it doesn't hurt them as much as it hurt the original convicts.

Throughout its long and chequered history New South Wales has proved itself to be a state always looking towards the future with its promise of even better times to come. This is as true today as it has always been, making New South Wales an exciting place to live in and to visit. It is surely the greatest state in Australia.

Facing page, top and bottom Timbertown, Wauchope.

The coast north of Sydney is a varied and beautiful area. *Left* the well-developed resort of The Entrance. *Top* Newcastle, the seventh largest city in Australia. *Above* Nelson Bay beach and *facing page, top and bottom* Nelson Bay harbour. Nelson Bay is the main town in Port Stephens and offers fine fishing.

The Blue Mountains have much to offer the visitor. Scenic Skyway *top* gives views of the Wentworth Falls *above and facing page*. Weeping Rock *right* is another attraction near to the skyway.

Many of the hills around Sydney are riddled with limestone caves of great beauty and elegance, the result of centuries of erosion by water running through the hills. The Kanangra Plateau *top and above* contains the famous Jenolan Caves. Blue Lagoon *right* stands near to the Grand Arch *facing page.*

ONE LANE SUBWAY
SWITCH ON LIGHTS
SLOW 15
SOUND HORN

Bathurst stands on the Great Western Highway, some 200 kilometres from Sydney. The old town is full of interesting sights. The finest public building in the town is probably the Court House *above*, built in 1880. The Mount Panorama Motor Racing Circuit *top* is the home of the James Hardie 1000. *Above left* St Stanislau's College. *Left and facing page, top* George Street. *Facing page, bottom* the Civic Centre.

JOHN MATTHEWS & CO.
thrift CHEMISTS
CHINESE INN
RESTAURANT
CAFE
JEWELLERS
MMI
FINANCE LIMITED
JOAN DEE LADIES WEAR
John Matthews & Co.
CHEMISTS

WOOLWORTHS

John Manny CHEMIST
AGENT FOR THE PRODUCTS OF
oul Pattinson
CAKES
AGE ROLLS
Soulcolor
Soul Pattinson CHEMIST
Sportsgirl
Sportsgirl
St. George
WILLIAMS
HE SHOEMEN

Although Dubbo *these pages* has only been a city since 1966, settlement dates back to the 1820s. Macquarie Street *facing page, top and bottom* is one of the city's more important thoroughfares and contains Old Dubbo Gaol *above, top left and top right* which dates back over a century. *Right* the War Memorial.

COBAR
PASTORAL
MINING
AND
TECHNOLOGICAL MUSEUM

Cobar *facing page,* deep inland on the Barrier Highway *top,* is a copper-mining town which produces half a million tonnes of ore a year. White Cliffs *above and right* lies even further west and has a population of just 150. Beautiful opals are mined here in small dug-outs, such as that *above.*

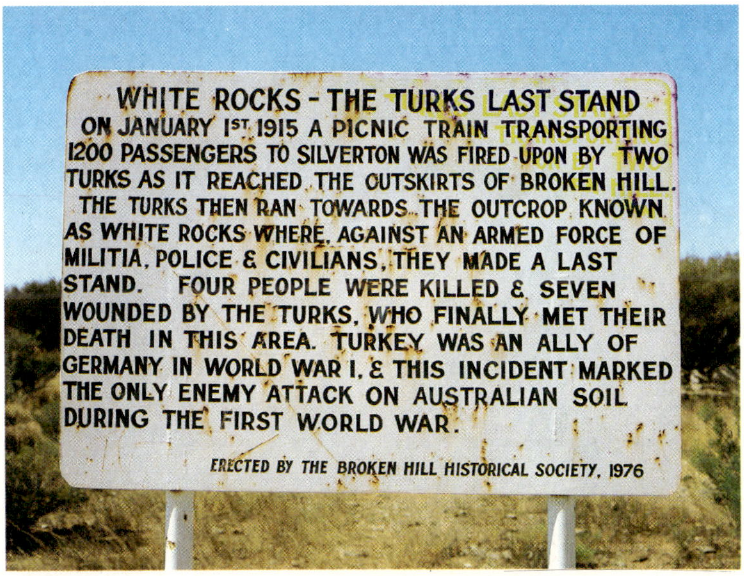

As the land spreads westwards from the Dividing Range it becomes more desert-like. The scenes *facing page* typify the land around Broken Hill *this page*. Broken Hill owes its existence to the area's incredibly rich deposits of silver, lead and zinc. The plate *above* tells the story of White Rocks *left*.

The mining town of Broken Hill has many fine buildings including the Court House *left*, the Post Office *above and top*, the Town Hall *top* and the Council Administrative Centre *facing page, bottom*. *Facing page, top* Sulphide Street Railway Station.

BROKEN HILL
SULPHIDE ST

Centre left the control centre and *top left* a plane for the NSW Flying Doctor Service. *Above, top right* and *centre right* the ghost town of Silverton. *Right* and *facing page* the restored Silverton Gaol.

GENERAL OFFICE
NO SMOKING

Around Griffith in New South Wales is an area known as the Murrumbidgee Miracle. The land was once little different from the rest of the New South Wales outback, but the name Murrumbidgee means 'never failing water' and that was the secret of success. In 1906 Parliament approved the construction of a massive irrigation scheme. Today, the scheme has grown to include more than half a million hectares of land and supports a population of some 50,000. Grapes are one of the area's most prolific crops, a large proportion of them going to the wine industry.

The Murrumbidgee Irrigation Area *facing page, top and bottom* is centred around Griffith. *Right and above right* Banner Avenue in Griffith. *Top* a bank and *above* the Memorial Gardens in Narrandera.

Long ago – more than 30,000 years – back in the Dreamtime, Aborigines lived and hunted in the region that is now Canberra. The first white settlers came here in the 1820s, not long after the original landings in the area of Sydney.

The Limestone Plains were discovered in 1820 by Wild, Smith and Vaughan. The first permanent settlement in the area of Canberra was the Canberry Station of Joshua Moore. Today, Canberra's hospital stands on this site. The oldest homestead in the region is *Duntroon*, which belonged to Robert Campbell and was built in 1833. Campbell received the first land grant and named his property after a castle in Scotland. This became the Royal Military College of Australia in 1911.

Canberra is 'the showplace of a nation'. Situated in the Molonglo Valley, its majestic setting and magnificent buildings constantly remind the visitor and the resident that this is the throbbing heart of a great nation. However, unlike other capital cities, it does not overawe people with forbidding fronts and miles of concrete. Hundreds of acres of parks and lawns are scattered throughout the city and the streets are wide and inviting. The sense of belonging and friendliness gained by walking the streets of Canberra is the result of careful planning. The city was planned to be beautiful; Walter Burley Griffin, who won the international competition for its design in 1912, said: "I have planned a city not like any other city in the world".

At the turn of the century the national capital was at Melbourne and the Molonglo Valley was a wild landscape dotted with gum trees and the occasional settlement. Following the inauguration of the Commonwealth, it was decided that a new capital was needed that was not associated with either of the two great rivals; Sydney and Melbourne. Consequently, in 1899, the 2,330 square kilometres around the stockmen's settlement of Canberry was set aside for the new capital. Many names were suggested for the proud national capital; including Mathilda, Utopia and Marsupiala; but, fortunately, the present name was chosen instead. This name, Canberra, was derived from the name of the stockmen's settlement which, in its turn, developed from the local Aboriginal name which meant 'place of meeting'. Surely a most apt name for the national capital.

After several years of foot dragging on the part of the government, an international competition was launched to find a design for the new city. The contest was won by the American architect Walter Burley Griffin and work began in 1913. His design embodied the blending of nature and construction, in a city where empty space was as important as buildings. Unfortunately, the Great War brought yet more delays and the passing of time meant alterations to Griffin's original design. Disillusioned, Griffin resigned. He never lived to see the completion of his dream. He died at the early age of 51 when he fell off some scaffolding.

But the work continued without him and, on May 9th, 1927, the federal Parliament was officially moved to the new city, amid great ceremony. But, once again, government departments were slow to act. Reluctant to leave the conveniences of the large cities, the civil servants did not move to Canberra until Robert Menzies insisted on it in 1955.

Today, Canberra is one of the most rapidly growing cities in Australia with a population currently over 220,000, and projected to reach half a million by the end of the century. The greatest industry is, of course, government; its departments and various spin-offs are the largest employers in the city, but tourism is also booming in importance, with more and more visitors each year. And there is plenty for them to see.

Flowing through the heart of the city is the Molonglo River, this has been dammed to create an artificial lake where yachts are sailed and canoes paddled. Near one end of the lake lies Aspen Island, which is the site of the famous 53-bell Carillon. This three-column

Facing page the Captain Cook Memorial, Canberra.

Overleaf Canberra from the air.

tower was presented to Canberra by the British Government to mark the city's 50th anniversary. The centre of the city, indeed its *raison d'être*, is the Parliament House. This attractive, white building is open to visitors whenever Parliament is not in session. It faces the Australian War Memorial, which lies on the other side of Lake Burley Griffin, at the head of ANZAC Parade. This impressive memorial was erected to the memory of those who died in many conflicts and houses a magnificent collection of paintings and relics of war. It is designed in a stylised Byzantine-style of architecture; the dome is covered in copper; the floor area is of 12,959 square metres and the building stands on the lower slopes of Mt Ainslie amid 12.14 hectares of terraced lawns.

Lake Burley Griffin may be regarded as the centrepiece of Canberra. It was made in 1963 with 35 km of shoreline, which is edged by beautiful trees, gardens and lawns. The area includes the Australian American Memorial, which consists of an aluminium shaft weighing 90 tonnes, standing 67 metres high, surrounded by a globe and eagle together adding 3.5 tonnes and 11 metres to the memorial's size. Near Commonwealth Avenue Bridge is the Captain Cook Memorial Jet, which throws water skywards for 140 metres. Also, on Regatta Point, is the Canberra Planning Exhibition.

Opened in 1927, Parliament House is ringed by beautiful lawns, rose gardens and fountains. The main public area is King's Hall, which was named after King George V. Key figures in the Federation of Australia are acknowledged here on bronze plaques. The National Library of Australia was opened in 1968 and is generally regarded as one of the most resplendent and graceful buildings in Australia. It is surrounded by forty-four columns which are faced with white Italian Carrare marble. The Australian National University is set amid wonderful natural surroundings. Here, the copper-covered dome of the Australian Academy of Science rests upon arches which rise out of a circular moat.

There are many other places of interest, both spectacular and homely, to see in this wonderful city as well as some of the best restaurants and parks in the country. The Botanic Gardens well express the essential spirit of the city, and contain some 6,000 indigenous plants, representing 2,000 species.

Spacious, elegant Canberra, built around the magnificent artificial lake and standing within the Australian Capital Territory is more than just the seat of Australia's government, it is the shining showplace of a youthful, forward-looking nation.

Facing page, top Lanyon, near Tharwa.

Facing page, bottom Blundell's Farmhouse, Canberra.

Top left the Canberra Carillon, on Aspen Island, consists of 53 bells and was presented by the British Government in honour of the city's golden jubilee. *Left* the Australian-American Memorial. *Top right* the telecommunications tower on Black Mountain. *Above* Mount Stromlo Observatory accurately provides the time service for Australia. *Facing page* Canberra Deep Space Communication Complex at Tidbinbilla. *Overleaf* views across Canberra.

These pages the Australian National Gallery and the Sculpture Garden which adorns its grounds with striking images in bronze and stainless steel.

Canberra *these pages* is the national capital of Australia. The city was designed by Walter Burley Griffin as the 'showplace of the nation'. *Left* the National Library, *facing page, bottom* the coat of arms outside the Law Courts. *Above, top and facing page, top* Parliament House. *Overleaf* the vacation snowfields of the Perisher Valley.

PUBLIC ENTRANCE
PUBLIC ENTRANCE
PUBLIC ENTRANCE
PUBLIC ENTRANCE

AUSTRALIA

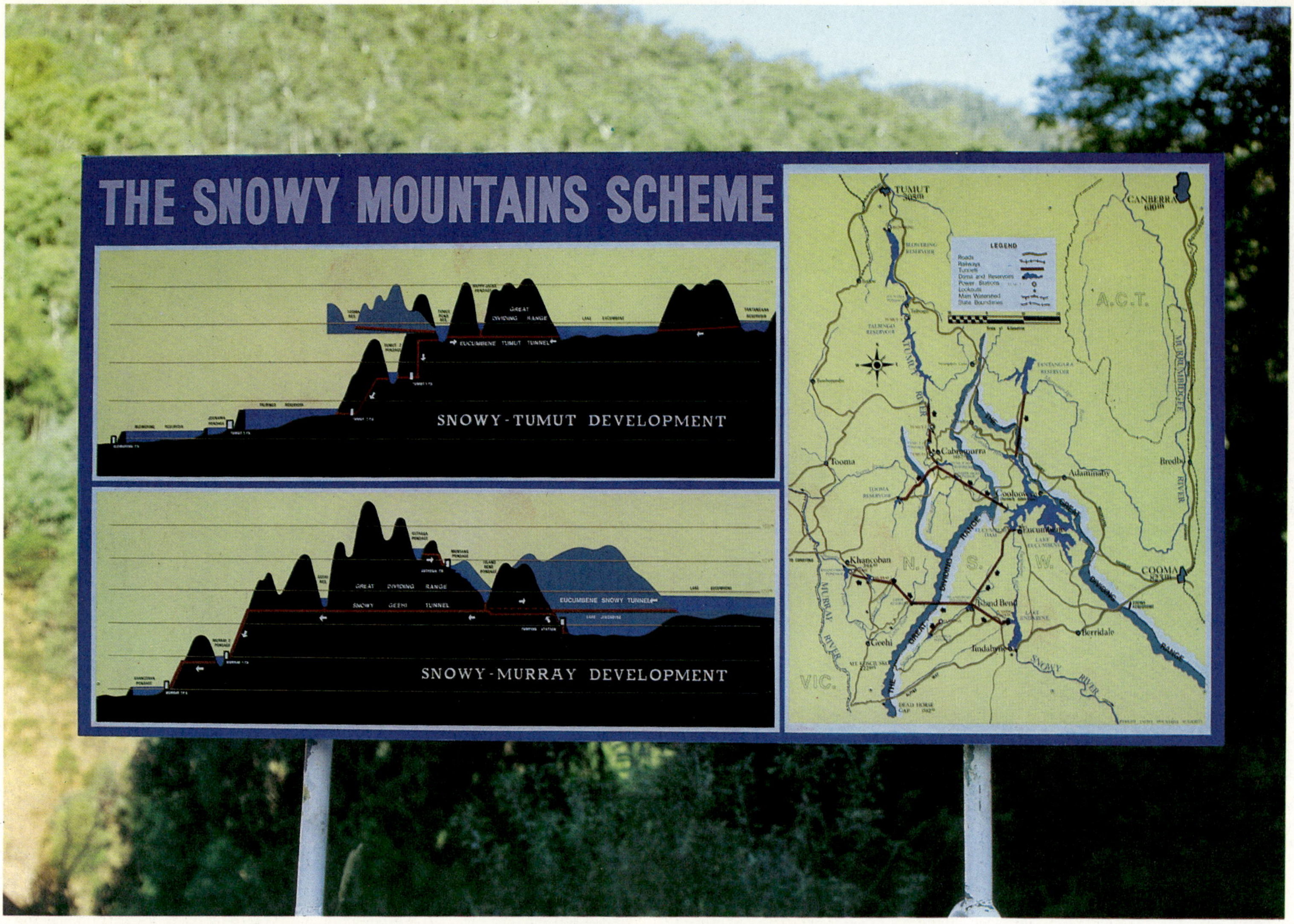

The Snowy Mountains Scheme, detailed *top*, is a vast hydro-electric project. Thredbo has a fine hotel *above left*. A statue *facing page* celebrates trout fishing at Adaminaby. *Left* a statue of 'the Man from Snowy River', Cooma. *Overleaf: top left and bottom left* the Clyde River Bridge at Batemans Bay; *top right* coal storage yard at Wollongong Docks and *bottom right* Port Kembla.

Covering an area only one-thirtieth of Australia's landmass – about the size of England, Scotland and Wales combined – the State of Victoria yet contains more than a quarter of the national population. It is the 'Garden State' of this island continent.

Before 1939 most of Victoria's population was native born, and even by 1947 only 8.7 per cent of the population was from abroad, mostly from Great Britain. Since the end of the Second World War, Victoria, in particular, has employed a policy of encouraging migration on a large scale from Europe. This was in keeping with the rest of Australia, and had the desired effect of reducing economic problems that were due to the low birth rate between the wars, as well as helping to provide a home for refugees from the battlefields of Europe and also making Australia stronger strategically.

By the time A.D. 2000 comes there may well be a state population of 8,000,000. This will probably accentuate the current regional disparities of density. At the moment some two-thirds of the people live in the area of Melbourne. Another 7 per cent live in four other urban developments with more than 20,000 inhabitants: Ballarat, Moe-Yallourn, Bendigo and Geelong, while a further 13 per cent live in another 113 towns which have under 20,000 people. This leaves only about 13 per cent of Victorians living in rural areas. The least dense rural areas are in the dry Mallee and the Alpine regions of the Eastern Highlands; the densest rural regions being in the dairylands of Gippsland and along the Murray Valley, where the fields benefit from irrigation.

Victoria can be divided into five main geographical regions – the western and central regions, the Grampians, Gippsland and the north-east Alpine region – but, for the visitor, it is divided into smaller areas by the Regional Tourist Authority. They not only deal with travellers, but also anyone who wants to develop new facilities for the area, as well as businesses that need assistance in the local region. Perhaps we can look at a few of these now to get a flavour of the disparate delights of Victoria.

The upland core of the state is in the **Central Highlands**. The explorer Major Mitchell came through the western part in 1836 and just one year later, flock-master Thomas Learmonth viewed the excellent grazing ground near present-day Ballarat. The stage was set for sheep rearing on a vast scale.

In 1851, an Irish prospector by the name of James Esmond found gold at Clunes. In the gold rush that followed, further discoveries were made at Buninyong, Ballarat, Smeaton, Beaufort, Creswick, Talbot and Ararat. Gold brought prosperity, and although alluvial deposits were almost exhausted by 1882, reef mining continued until 1918.

In Ballarat is found the site of the Eureka Stockade. It was here on December 3, 1854, that the only rebellion in Australia's history was fought by miners protesting over problems associated with mining licences. They were quickly defeated by soldiers.

The **Westernport-Healesville** region is where mountain, sea and shore meet under the sun. Never more than 150 kilometres from Melbourne, this area is where relaxation comes in many forms. On the beaches of Westernport Bays or Port Phillip you can while your cares away, or watch fishing boats ply their way through the sea.

Phillip Island was discovered in 1798 by George Bass. Besides the unspoilt pleasures of the beach, around Kitty Miller Bay you can fossick for gemstones. Each year a million people come to this island paradise, where one of the attractions is the sight of penguins tumbling from the sea as dusk falls, to parade past the watching tourists. Here on this island can also be seen large colonies of koalas among the manna gums.

The contrast of the **Otway-Geelong** region is from its flat, fertile plains to the sudden rising of its granite ranges. In 1802, Matthew Flinders landed at Indented Head and climbed the peaks of the You Yangs. Nearby, at Point Lonsdale, there is a cave where an escaped convict, William Buckley, took refuge with the Aborigines for 32 years, becoming known as "the wild white man".

Facing page the Post Office at Geelong.

surveying error it was claimed by both South Australia and Victoria, the argument lasting for fifty years. Another problem was that during this time smuggling was big business between the two colonies and any law-breakers in the area would claim to belong to the other state to avoid arrest. The dungeons at Serviceton can still be seen, the railway station having filled the dual role of gaol and mortuary.

Near Brim can be seen parts of the original Wild Dog Fence built between Swan Hill and the South Australian border in 1885-86. There is also the Glenorchy Presbyterian Church, 112 years old but in use to this day. The Ebenezer Mission Church at Antwerp, near Dimboola, stands as a reminder of the efforts of missionaries from Moravia, Czechoslovakia, to look after the shrinking population of local Aborigines. The mortal remains of these good people lie in the graveyard alongside those of the Aborigines they tried to help.

The **Murray** was described by Captain Sturt as "a broad and noble river". For 2,500 kilometres it winds its way through countryside of the greatest magnificence. Superb lakeland scenery and a tremendous variety of wildlife make the Murray Valley a fascinating area of natural beauty.

The ecosystem in this area is a wonderland for the naturalist. There are many species of water birds such as swans, ducks, egrets, bitterns, coots, grebes and herons. Yarrawonga itself derives its name from the Aborigine title meaning "nesting place of cormorants". Above the waters are sea-eagles, harriers and kites. Parrots and cockatiels flit through the woodland. In the bush itself can be found kangaroos, echidnas, emus and possums.

The Murray Valley produces many fine wines such as the well-known Rutherglen vintages, however, there are also some Lake Country wineries which produce good wines. Lake Boga, Woorinen, Beverford and Wood Wood are examples, and lower down there is the McWilliam's winery at Robinvale. The Mildara winery at Merbein, near Mildura, stands high above the Murray.

A fine view is obtainable from Mt Wycheproof which, at 42.5 metres high, is referred to by local people as the "lowest mountain in the world".

Victoria is a state of immense variety, from the area of the **North West**, to the **South West** and over to **East Gippsland**. And between these lies the fair **Melbourne** region.

Melbourne is perhaps the most elegant city of Australia. Graceful, broad boulevards sweep through the centre of the city, echoing the Yarra River's tree-lined curves. In the heart of this capital city of the state lie some of the world's most glorious gardens. The Royal Botanic and Alexandra Gardens are the delight of visitors and horticulturalists alike. Likewise, for admirers of art and culture Melbourne is unsurpassed; ballet, theatre and the arts all seek to draw your attention.

The tough pioneers who came here in 1835, led by John Batman, established the settlement of Beargrass. When he arrived from Tasmania, Batman purchased 343,000 hectares from the local Aborigines and set up both houses and stores. Within three years these humble beginnings had expanded into a town; then by 1837 it received its first government administrator and its new name – Melbourne.

The town's development progressed at a reasonable rate, eventually becoming a city, until the year 1851. This was the time when Victoria was declared to be separate from New South Wales and hence from the centre of government in Sydney. Realising how momentous this decision was, and what its future effect would be on their city, the inhabitants celebrated by having a picnic! But there was to be another tremendous upheaval for Melbourne in the same year – gold was discovered at Bendigo and Ballarat, a hundred miles inland. As the news reached the citizens, the city became a ghost town as they downed tools and went out to chance their hands searching for the yellow metal of their dreams.

However, as word spread far and wide, prosperity also came the way of Melbourne itself through the influx of new prospectors – 100,000 in 1852 alone – as virtually all supplies for

Facing page Apollo Bay. *Overleaf* the coastline of Port Campbell National Park.

the mines came from the city. By 1854 the size of Melbourne's population was 80,000 people. So, in the wake of gold came prosperity, increasing trade and industry. By 1880 there was a rail link to Ballarat, Bendigo, Geelong and Wodonga, and in 1883 this was patched into the rail network of New South Wales at Albury. As the century drew to a close, Melbourne was a business and industrial centre to be reckoned with throughout the continent, having a population of 300,000.

Today, the city holds well over two million people and covers 6,000 square kilometres. It is the dominant force in Victoria, both socially and economically. Not to be wondered at really, considering that this port is at the hub of the state's communication system and its centre of population.

The port itself covers 25 square kilometres around the mouth of the Yarra River. Any of the major exports from Victoria pass through here, whether wool, meat, fruit, the various dairy products or metals, so providing employment and prosperity for the work force. Imports also have to come via the port: oil, coal, iron and chemicals. Beyond Melbourne, of course, there is immense interest in the wealth below the waters of Bass Strait.

For those who seek culture there is no shortage of things to do. The splendid National Gallery is the repository and showplace for one of the finest collections of art in the world, and the National Museum of Victoria as well as the Science Museum also boast fine collections. The music lover, too, is catered for, with a varied programme of free entertainment in the parks during summer months.

However, it is sport that is the passion for many. There are plenty of sports grounds and swimming pools, while the golden sands of the beaches are natural playgrounds for fun-lovers. Spectator sports draw the crowds as well and, of course, this includes the ever popular Australian Rules Football. Melbourne Cricket Ground can accomodate 110,000, and in this sports-minded city the first Tuesday of November is declared a public holiday so that everyone can watch the horse-race of the year, where riders compete for the prestigious Melbourne Cup.

Melbourne possesses a cosmopolitan flavour, probably due to the influx of migrants following the end of the Second World War. Signs adorn shops in Italian, Greek, Turkish or Italian and hearing many languages being spoken is common. A stream of people passes through Tullamarine International Airport, both from overseas and interstate. The Melbourne Heliport is used to ferry passengers to the airport to catch their flights. Chinatown provides a sense of the Orient set against the high-rise concrete skyline. The Chinese came here first in gold rush days and settled along Little Bourke Street.

The Moomba Festival in March is a colourful carnival, with sporting events, open-air art exhibitions, fireworks lighting up the night sky and lively processions through the streets.

Because of its wide streets, Melbourne has fortunately been able to retain its tramway system. Horse-drawn trams lasted until 1923 when the sheds that housed them were destroyed by fire. Cable trams were used for over 50 years, from 1885 until 1940.

Inside the Old Melbourne Gaol, Russell Street, which was commenced in 1841, is a museum containing the gallows. A sign alongside the gallows states that the rope was left hanging from the beam until the prisoner mounted the scaffold; the rope was then knotted tightly around his neck. It was here that the notorious Ned Kelly was executed in November 1880, and underneath the gallows can be seen the suit of armour that he wore during his infamous outlaw days.

Not far from Melbourne itself is the Dandenong Ranges, a spur of the Great Dividing Range, which overlooks the city and gives breathtaking views of this gateway to the riches of the State of Victoria.

Facing page the rugged coastline of Victoria. *Overleaf* Bridgewater Bay, near Portland.

Hamilton
Spectator
REAL ESTATE AGENTS
Australia Post
Antiques

EST. 1876
T&G
REECE BURGESS
PHARMACY
FOOD
TV
rental
TRAVEL

Hamilton *facing page, top* stands to the south of the Grampians region and Horsham *above and facing page, bottom* to the north.

Top the Victoria Hotel bar in Beulah. *Right* some of the abundant vineyards to be found around the town of Mildura.

Mildura stands on the Murray River, once the busiest waterway in Australia. Today, only a few riverboats, *this page* the *Coonawarra*, remain of the dozens that once plied the waters. Mildura is also known for the bar *facing page* in its Workingman's Club, said to be the world's longest.

NO STANDING
SERVICE ONLY

Mildura has much to offer the visitor and resident: *above* the world's largest Humpty Dumpty, *top and facing page, top* Deakin Avenue, *left* 8th Street and *facing page, bottom* the City Council Library.

Top winery near Red Cliffs. The Swan Hill Pioneer Settlement *remaining pictures* preserves many buildings and machines from the early days of settlement in Victoria.

PYAP
PYAP

PROFESSOR
MORTIMER'S
PHOTOGRAPHIC PARLOUR
POST OFFICE

PRIDE
MURRAY

Facing page, bottom salt ponds near Manangatang. Echuca *remaining pictures* grew up in the 1850s as an important river port, but by 1900 was in decline. The Goulburn irrigation project brought fresh prosperity to the surrounding agricultural area, for which Echuca serves as a centre. *Overleaf* Bendigo.

BENDIGO'S
VINTAGE 'TALKING' TRAM
TOUR.
LEAVES THIS POINT
TIME TABLE
TRAM TOUR
BENDIGO TRAMWAYS
Nº 30
LITTER

COLES
COLES
McCALMANS
GOLD COUNTRY RADIO
3CV
NO ENTRY

Sovereign Hill *these pages* is one of the most popular tourist attractions in Ballarat. It faithfully recreates the wild days of the gold rushes with stagecoaches, gold panning and replica buildings.

HALL
ROBINSON & WAYNE
GOLD OFFICE
COBB & CO

GOLD PANNING DEMONSTRATIONS

This page and overleaf
Puffing Billy offers scenic rides in the Dandenongs.
Facing page the *Polly*

Woodside, built in 1885, has been restored and cared for by the National Trust of Australia (Victoria).

POLLY WOODSIDE

GUARD
7A

STATE BANK

Melbourne is the elegant city of Australia. Broad, graceful boulevards sweep through the city centre seeming to echo the tranquil, tree-lined curve of the Yarra River which meanders to the sea. Set in the heart of the capital of the 'Garden State' are some of the most glorious gardens in the world. The 225 acres of the Royal Botanic and Alexandra Gardens are admired and respected by horticulturalists the world over. For lovers of art and culture Melbourne is unsurpassed on the continent; ballet, theatre and the arts jostle with each other for attention.

All this was far from the minds of the hardy pioneers, led by John Batman, who established the settlement of Bearbrass in 1835. Arriving from Tasmania, Batman purchased 343,000 hectares from the local Doutgalla tribe of Aborigines for an annual tribute of goods which was worth about £200, and established stores and houses there. Batman wrote in his diary of the place where the Old Customs House was to be built, "this will be the place for a village". Within three years the group of buildings he had founded had grown into a town and, in 1837, it received its first government administrator and a new name – Melbourne. This was in honour of Lord Melbourne, the British Prime Minister.

The development of the area proceeded steadily but slowly until 1851, when two momentous events rocked the city. First the colony of Victoria was declared to be separate from New South Wales and so from government by Sydney. The importance of this event was at once recognised by the inhabitants of Melbourne who celebrated by having a picnic. The second major event of the year was the discovery of gold at Bendigo and Ballarat, a hundred miles inland. When news of the discovery reached Melbourne nearly everyone left the city, which became a virtual ghost town. But as more and more prospectors arrived from around the world, 100,000 in 1852 alone, Melbourne cashed in on the boom in trade. Virtually all the supplies for the mining towns came through the city. Fortunes and the population boomed; by 1854 Melbourne counted 80,000 people among its inhabitants. With the increase in trade, population and prosperity which came in the wake of the gold there also grew industry, the more stable indication of a city's growth. By 1880 Melbourne was linked by rail to Ballarat, Bendigo, Geelong and Wodonga and in 1883 this rail network was finally linked with the system in New South Wales at Albury. By the 1880s, the well-known British journalist, George Augustus Sala, was referring to the city as "Marvellous Melbourne". By the close of the century Melbourne was a thriving business and industrial centre with a population of 300,000. Her future was assured.

Today, Melbourne is a bustling city of well over two million people and covers over 270,000 hectares. It dominates the economic and social life of Victoria, which is hardly surprising in view of its population and position at the centre of the communications network. The great port, in essence the city's *raison d'être*, covers some twenty-five square kilometres around the mouth of the Yarra River (the Aborigine word *Yarra* means "swiftly moving"). The major exports of the entire state pass through here; these are wool, metals, meat, fruit and numerous dairy products, providing much of the employment and economic vitality of the city. Imports, in the shape of oil, coal, chemicals and iron, pour into the state through Melbourne.

As the capital of the state, Melbourne is the focus for the social and cultural life of Victoria's far-flung population. Theatre and the arts flourish, the National Gallery houses one of the finest art collections in the world, while orchestral concerts are a great feature of the city's nightlife. The restaurants and hotels of Melbourne are justly famous for the excellence of their cuisine and the elegance of their settings.

But perhaps the favourite pastime of the inhabitants of the city where trams still run on rails, is sport. Spread throughout the city are dozens of sports grounds and swimming

Facing page Melbourne's Flinders Street Station and the Yarra.

Overleaf Melbourne's trams.

CAGA
THE SALVATION ARMY
SAFETY ZONE
KEEP LEFT
MMTB
BUSES EXCEPTED

HOYTS
THE CINEMA CENTRE
RESTAURANT
IMPERIAL HOTEL
97
North Fitzroy
209

pools, while the nearby beaches are natural playgrounds. But it is spectator sports which pull the greatest crowds; the tough game of Australian Rules Football, "Aussie Rules", is one of the most popular and is played in the winter months, attracting up to 60,000 people for Saturday matches and 120,000 for the finals. The game is rather loosely based upon the rough game of Gaelic football. The 1892 Cup final was attended by 67,000 people, which was headline news in the then daily *Argus* as there was only a population of 500,000 in the entire city. For other fans the Melbourne Cricket Ground can hold 110,000 spectators. Sport is such a feature of life in the city that the first Tuesday of November is declared a public holiday so that the population can attend the Melbourne Cup; the greatest horse race of the year. The entire nation waits upon the result of the event which takes place at the Flemington race course.

Moomba time comes to Melbourne every year in March. The festival lasts for ten days and the word Moomba means "lets get together and have fun". However, fun awaits people every day in Melbourne. You can sample the delights of Dutch, German, Italian, Greek, Asian or French cooking. As a well-known centre of fashion, the shopping stores and arcades are of the finest calibre. The theatre was flourishing soon after the original settlement was made, including open-air theatre at St Kilda. The lavish decoration adorning the Comedy, Princess and Her Majesty's recalls those days gone by of the theatre's heyday in Melbourne. There are plenty of nightspots to delight the visitor, and there are fine examples of ballet, music, opera and the arts.

Mention must be made of the annual Melbourne Film Festival. This is an example of the state of the cinema in the city which regularly shows all the latest national productions, as well as those from America, Asia and Europe. In 1945, the State Film Centre was formed, showing a variety of feature films and documentaries, and possesses a library which has amassed over 20,000 films to date.

The city of Melbourne is intrinsically a great place, rich in culture and entertainments. But it is not only its own attractions that exclusively feature – it is also the gateway to Victoria, the 'Garden State', which although the smallest state on the continent at 227,620 square kilometres, has almost one-third of Australia's total population.

Facing page Bourke Street Mall.

Overleaf Royal Arcade.

RÖGER DAVID

Knit'n'Wool
CENTRE
Statewide
YOUNG MADAM
FASHIONS & SPORTSWEAR
TRAVEL SERVICE
GOLD STAMPING
SHARPENING
KEYS CUT
ENGRAVING ENGRAVING ENGRAVING
60 SECOND SERVICES

pb
Shoes
Games
Parlour
House Of
Kali
ITALIAN
SHOES
WINTER SALE WINTER SALE

MYER HOUSE
Airport West
59
171
LONSDALE ST
MISSIONS
michaels

MLC
SEC
EXTRA MILD

Flinders Street Station *top and facing page, bottom* lies at the centre of the state's rail network. Trains are not the only form of transport to run on rails in Melbourne. The tram system *above and facing page, top* has been in operation for over a century. *Overleaf* the Bourke Street Mall.

MYER
COLES STORES

CHINA
CUTLERY
GIFTS
ROYAL ARCADE
ROYAL ARCADE
DUNKLINGS

Melbourne has many exciting and unusual buildings within its boundaries: the Exhibition Building *facing page, top,* the Princess Theatre *right,* the Sidney Myer Music Bowl *below* and the Victorian Arts Centre *facing page, bottom.* But perhaps the most important of them all is the very ordinary-looking cottage shown *bottom left.* In this cottage lived a small boy who would one day discover Australia – James Cook. The cottage was recently shipped from England in pieces and rebuilt.

DELI

Previous pages Collins Place, a modern, shopping and business complex. The tempting restaurants and colourful architecture of Little Bourke Street *left* and *above* have their origins in the gold rushes, when many Chinese coolies came to Victoria. *Facing page* Flinders Street Station.

SEC
HELLO YELLOW 1984
federation insurance
OPEN SUNDAY

BENSON and HEDGES
3:06
Coca-Cola
SEC
federation insurance
473

The first settlers came to the Yarra from Tasmania in 1835. Led by John Batman, they journeyed in search of farmland and a new life. Bearbrass – the primitive settlement that they founded – prospered and, by the 1850s, elegant mansions were being built. One of these, Como, is shown *these pages.* Overlooking the Yarra River, the stately rooms and grounds remind visitors of an age when life was more relaxed and refined. The building is now cared for by the National Trust of Australia (Victoria).

The people of Melbourne are well known for their love of the outdoors, perhaps the greatest expression of which is beachlife *these pages.* Around Port Phillip Bay are many sandy beaches where the citizens can relax. *Left* Elwood Beach, *remaining pictures* Brighton Beach and *overleaf* Sandringham Beach.

Victoria's historic past is evidenced throughout the state by the carefully preserved homes of the early settlers, as shown *above, above right and facing page, bottom. Top* the spillway dam of Lake Eildon. The land around the lake is typified *facing page, top,* near the Howqua River.

HAIRDRESSER
R. ROSEN

WATCHMAKER
AND
JEWELLER
FLORIST

Beechworth *these pages,* west of Lake Hume, is one of the largest towns in the region. *Above, top and facing page, top* Tanswell's Hotel in Ford Street, *left* the Post Office and its well-known clock tower and *facing page, bottom* shady walkways in Ford Street.

Mount Buffalo National Park *above and facing page* spreads out south of Myrtleford. Lake Buffalo *top* lies just to the west; *right* a nearby river.

Gippsland *these pages* is well known for its beaches and lakes. At the eastern end of the magnificent 90 Mile Beach *top* is Lakes Entrance *above and right*. Further inland, lightning streaks the sky near Sale *facing page, top. Facing page, bottom* Yarram.

GENERAL STORE
Coca-Cola
BAIT SUPPLY
MILK BAR
Coca-Cola
Peters
ice
ICE

This page Coal Creek Historical Park near Korumburra is a recreation of a coal mining town from around the turn of the century.

Facing page Wilsons Promontory National Park is one of the largest and most beautiful in the state. *Top* Squeaky Beach and *bottom* Whisky Bay.

Phillip Island, at the mouth of Western Port Bay: *facing page, bottom* Pyramid Rock and *facing page, top* Woolamai Beach. *Top* Bourne Creek.

The holiday island state of Tasmania lies about 240 km south of the State of Victoria, from which it is separated by Bass Strait. This shallow strip of water was a land bridge between 25 and 40 million years ago. The independent character of Tasmania's people is reflected in the classic headline in one of the island's newspapers: "Fog in Bass Straight – Mainland Cut Off"!

The state comprises the island of Tasmania itself, with several smaller islands off its coast; Bruny Island, close to Hobart the capital; King and Flinders islands and, 1,000 miles to the southeast, subantarctic Macquarie Island. Having the second highest rainfall in Australia, Tasmania has a dense growth of vegetation. The temperature ranges from 14-25 degrees centigrade in summer to 5-16 degrees in winter. Snow is plentiful above 1,000 metres in July and August.

Tasmania has an area of about 68 million hectares and is 296 km long by 314 km wide, which is about the size of Scotland. However, its population is less than half a million people. The land is essentially mountainous and is dominated by the glaciated and lake-covered Central Plateau which rises to nearly 1,200 metres, with several peaks above 1,500 metres. Valleys and ridges run parallel to one another in a northwest – southeast direction. In the west and southwest, there are thousands of hectares of country that have yet to be explored on the ground. Except for those relatively flat areas of land cleared for agricultural use, most of Tasmania is covered by dense vegetation. Large tracts of the southwest are covered by the dreaded 'horizontal' (*Anodopetalum*) which grows in such a matted manner that it can only be cut by skilled axemen or prospectors using power saws.

The first European to discover Tasmania was the Dutch navigator, Abel Janszoon Tasman, who made landfall on the west coast in November 1642. He named the island "Van Diemen's Land" after the governor of the Dutch East Indies. A French captain, Marion du Fresne, sighted the island in 1772, and it was five more years before Captain Cook landed at Adventure Bay on Bruny Island. Later, when spies told Governor King in New South Wales that French officers were planning to settle Van Diemen's Land, the British dispatched an expedition there. A settlement was formed at Risdon Cove, up the Derwent River, in 1803, and the island was formally annexed by Great Britain the following year. Unfortunately, it became a penal colony for the hardened prisoners. The governor wrote in his diary in 1824, "My discipline is such that the entire colony...is run as one gaol"! Some managed to escape to the bush: Matthew Brady succeeded in this and took to robbing the rich, giving to the poor and cheekily put up 'wanted' posters, with 25 gallons of rum reward for the capture of the governor, Sir George Arthur. It was this governor who was responsible for trying to herd the native Aborigines into one corner of the island. They resisted the seizure of their tribal lands and were gradually exterminated. In 1835, evangelist George Robinson took 187 surviving members of the race to Flinders Island. But they did not thrive and in 1876 the last one, a woman known as Queen Truganini, died.

Today, the economy of Tasmania is mainly agricultural, although secondary industries account for a large sector. Half of Australia's tin production comes from here. Mining is also carried out for zinc, iron-ore, silver and scheelite, which is the ore of tungsten. Although Tasmania has only 3 per cent of Australia's population, it provides more than 10 per cent of its electricity through hydroelectric power.

More than 200,000 people visit Tasmania each year. The temperate summer climate is ideal when wandering through the beautiful countryside, or along the streets of historic Hobart with its Georgian buildings. Named after Robert Hobart, Fourth Earl of Buckinghamshire and Secretary of State for the Colonies, the city is dominated by majestic Mt Wellington, rising up 1,250 metres with its forested slopes, and snow-

Facing page Tasman Bridge.

Overleaf Hobart from Lindisfarne.

covered for much of the year. As a busy port, Hobart has a strong seafaring tradition going back to early whaling days. The finish of the ever-popular Sydney to Hobart yacht race can be seen here at New Year. The capital also has the first casino to have been licensed on the Australian continent; the Wrest Point Casino, which provides from its revolving restaurant a lovely view of the harbour and its surrounds. There is a wonderful floor show and the gambling facilities are excellent. The latter includes the Australian game of 'two up'.

The oldest theatre in Australia can be found in Hobart; the Theatre Royal. There is also the Playhouse which puts on many local productions. There are plenty of art galleries and cinemas, which screen many locally made productions. Sports enthusiasts get plenty of encouragement and there are wonderful facilities for tennis players, footballers, followers of horse racing and boating. Outdoor sports in Tasmania also include swimming, surfing, water-skiing, skin diving, sailing, fishing, golf, bushwalking, trail riding and skiing.

Shopping in Hobart is a delight, with many top stores along its streets and arcades. In the main shopping area, opening off Cat and Fiddle Square, is the Cat and Fiddle Arcade. Here is found, set among surrounds of tree and fountain, a kinetic mural reflecting the nursery rhyme of the same name, which chimes each hour. The city is also rich in restaurants, including dishes of a local flavour which are sometimes influenced by Hobart's maritime position. Hobart enjoys a special character – a mixture of old-world charm and thrusting modernism.

There are many beautiful National Parks to visit in Tasmania which are rich in fauna. Mammals include the brush and ringtail possum and the wallaby. Among the marsupial carnivores are the Tasmanian devil, the native cat, tiger cat, and the rare thylacine. Fourteen species of birds are to be found only on this island including the Tasmanian native hen, dusky robin and green rosella.

It is no wonder that Tasmania, with its diversity and beauty, has won its place as a holiday island for Australians. This book captures all the colour and wonder of this land that has earned it the epithet of 'Treasure Island'.

Facing page cottages in Battery Point, Hobart.

Overleaf Hobart and Mount Wellington by night.

itp
INCOME TAX
SSIONALS
walkin Shoes
lowest prices
ELLISON HAWKER
LOTTERIES
MYER
INCOME TAX
CHRISTMAS PAGEANT

ZGERALD
FITZGERALDS
THROUGHOUT TASMANIA
FITZGERALDS
TO CAT & FIDDLE SQUARE
FITZGERALDS
MENSWEAR
FITZGERALDS

Previous pages Hobart from Mount Nelson. *Facing page: top* Liverpool Street and *bottom* Elizabeth Street Mall. *Top* Collins Street, *above* Franklin Square and *right* Salamanca Place. *Overleaf* Tasman Bridge.

FINALE

Previous pages Wrest Point Marina and Casino in Hobart. *These pages* the rugged landscapes of western Tasmania, where mountains and dense rainforests abound. *Top* Lake Gordon and the Gordon Dam. *Left and above* on Russell Falls, Mount Field National Park. *Facing page* the mountains of Queenstown.

JIMMY'S
A.F. MURRAY & SONS
LIQUORLAND
JANE
ART

CLAYTONS
WALLPAPER
Clark
MAPLES

Previous pages the city of Launceston lies on the Tamar River in northern Tasmania. Just outside Launceston is spectacular Cataract Gorge *above and facing page, top,* as well as the Gunpowder Mill *left, top and facing page, bottom.* Set within an old quarry, it is part of the famous Penny Royal Complex; one of the city's major tourist attractions.

Facing page Tasman Arch on the Tasman Peninsula, where the ruins of the Port Arthur penal settlement – the church *top*, the asylum *centre right* and the penitentiary *right* – are a poignant reminder of the past. *Above* the historic church of Saint John the Baptist in Buckland, 50km north of Port Arthur.

Facing page Devils Kitchen on the Tasman Peninsula. Built by convicts in 1823, across the Coal River, Richmond Bridge *above and top* is one of the many interesting historic structures in the town, such as the courtyard of Richmond gaol *left*.

BANK
NATIONAL
AMP

JOHN MARTINS
REGENT
CINEMA 1
CINEMA 2

Because of its design it is easy to see Adelaide on foot, as the principal buildings are all contained within a small area of the city centre. Among the places of interest to see are the State War Memorial; Government House, set in an area of lawns and gardens; the Museum of Natural History; the State Library; the Art Gallery of South Australia; the National Gallery; St Peter's Anglican Cathedral; Holy Trinity Church of England; the University of Adelaide and Parliament House.

Aside from the diversity of the city itself, it also acts as a gateway to the Flinders Ranges and the lower Murray Valley. Within a short distance of the city there are the Mount Lofty Ranges and Mount Lofty Summit only a thirty minute drive from the centre of Adelaide. From the top are spectacular views over the city and out to sea. Nearby are the Torrens Wild Flower Park and the Athelstone Wildflower Garden. It is also the start of an 800 km bush walk – the Heysen trail. Other places to visit are the Botanic Gardens and Park; the Cleland Conservation Park and Belair Recreation Park. With the residential and industrial areas outside the belt of parklands around Adelaide, the city centre is a lovely and charming place.

But Adelaide is not simply a beautiful city, it is a capital city; the centre of a thriving state that stretches from the Nullarbor Plain to the Murray Valley and from the Great Australian Bight to the heart of the Red Centre. Contained within the boundaries of the state are the secrets of Adelaide's prosperity. The city has acted as an exporting port for all the natural wealth of the state and as a focus for its financial life.

Perhaps the most delicious export produced by South Australia is that of the Barossa Valley; wine. Wine came to the Barossa with the Germans in the middle of the last century and the German traditions are still strong. There are churches, festivals and costumes strongly reminiscent of the old country throughout the valley. But the wines are not confined to German types. Diligent research has resulted in a fine selection of clarets, burgundies and even champagnes being available, especially during the Vintage Festival.

Adelaide is a beautiful city at the heart of a beautiful state. The superb collection of photographs in this book shows the city at its liveliest and most attractive.

Facing page Rundle Mall in Adelaide.

Overleaf Adelaide's Festival Centre.

As the capital of South Australia, Adelaide is the home of the Governor's Residence *top*. *Left and above* Hindmarsh Square with its elegant fountain.

Facing page, top Pulteney Street. *Overleaf* Rundle Mall where modern stores, market stalls and shady trees combine to create a beautiful shopping street.

THE BLOCK
TAILORING

SINGER
JANOME
SHOPPING

COFFEE SHOP
ADELAIDE ARCADE
HOYTS
CINEMA 1
CINEMA 2
ADELAIDE ARCADE
Radio Rentals
TRADING HOURS

REGENT
HARRIS SCARFE
Sportsgirl
Bank
ROGER DAVID
MARTINS
AUSTRALIA
Variety
Ezywalkin Shoes

IMFC
CAR PARK
RAFFLES
SUPPER CLUB
OF TOKYO
MONWEALTH
NOW SHOWING
FAIR LADY
CML
Adelaide
Valet Service
SAME DAY
DOWNTOWN

THE City HOTEL
POLITES
POLITES
SAUNA
ATHENS
The Shah

Previous pages Hindley Street at night possesses an exciting and cosmopolitan atmosphere. *Above* the Botanic Hotel. *Top, right and facing page* startling views of the Festival Centre. Set next to the Torrens River, it is home to the world-famous Adelaide Arts Festival. This is a wonderful celebration which displays the cultural excellence of the state. *Overleaf* Saint Peter's Cathedral.

AMP
Ansett.

This page the tranquil Torrens River provides rest and sport for Adelaide's joggers and rowers alike.

Facing page the bandstand adjacent to the Festival Centre. *Overleaf* Adelaide from Montefiore Park.

AMP
Ansett
BANK NATIONAL
SHELL

A few kilometres from Adelaide, on the South Road, is Morphett Vale. The town contains a recreation *these pages* of a pioneer settlement of the 1860s. The reconstruction is complete with a blacksmith's *facing page, bottom,* a thatched cottage *left* and horse-drawn carriages.

ESTD 1859
General Store
TEA MERCHANT & FANCY GOODS
CIGARETTES 10 for 3d
MONKEY
pay cash
ROYAL MAIL
COBB & CO.
POST OFFICE
GRIFFITHS BROS

JOHN HIGGINS
BLACKSMITH & FARRIER

These pages and overleaf just an hour's drive from Adelaide is the fertile Barossa Valley; Australia's foremost wine producing region. Although it is only 8km wide by 30km long, there is found here a lovely, quaint world of magnificent churches, imposing chateaux and tiny villages. The area was settled in the mid-19th century by Germans who had escaped religious persecution in their own country. Their cultural influence is still felt strongly today in this friendly valley.

The Barossa Valley *facing page* is famed for the quality of its fruits, in particular the grapes which are used to produce the well-known wines. The valley does not, however, have a monopoly on the fruit growing in South Australia. Riverland *this page* produces some two million tonnes of fruit each year, the result of successful irrigation. *Far left* lemons, *left* a fruit stall near Berri, *top left* oranges, *top right* fruit tree pruning and *above* pruning vines near Barmera.

OFFICE EQUIPMENT
NEWSAGENCY
LOTTERY TICKETS
LADIES
BANK
CHICKENS
TREVS

This page the Barossa Valley: *above and top left* Tanunda, *right* near Dorrien, *centre* the Kaiser Stuhl cellars, Nuriootpa, *top right* Chateau Yaldara. *Facing page, bottom* Waikerie and *facing page, top* a Murray ferry near Berri. *Overleaf* Gawler.

UFS-347

Townsend
PHARMACY
GAWLER ARMS
HOTEL

Moonta *this page* is one of the towns in the 'Little Cornwall' area on the Yorke Peninsula which boomed after the discovery of copper in 1861. Hundreds of miners from Cornwall, England, settled in the area, bringing their skills and culture. *Left* the Municipal Offices, *far left* Ellen St, *above* the Uniting Church in Australia, *above left* nearby derelict mine buildings, *top right* a miner's cottage and *top left* a house on Henry St. *Facing page, bottom* Moonta Bay and *facing page, top* nearby Port Hughes.

Iron Knob *facing page, top* is a massive ore mining operation in the desert interior of South Australia. It is linked to Whyalla by a railway *left and facing page, bottom* across miles of scrub *above. Top* the Lincoln Highway.

MERCURY
MERCURY
OUTBOARDS

Ceduna *the*
some 780 k
Adelaide, c
Highway. W
of over 2,0(
last town o
before the l
strikes out
Nullarbor I
Perth. The t
shallower w
Great Aust
where whit
great numb
acts as a sm
exporting g
right and cen
gypsum *bot*
Overseas T
Earth Static
which links
with Asia, /
Europe, lies
to the north

COMMONWEALTH
BANK
COMMONWEALT
BANKING CORP
PIZZA
RESTAURANT
CAFE
OPEN
WELCOME TO ALBANY
ESPLANADE MOTOR HOTEL
HAMMERS
CRAVEN
Special Mild
CRAVEN
Special Mild
DAILY NEWS
Betts&Betts

South of the Kimberley Plateau is one of the great wonders of the natural world. Wolf Creek Crater was formed many thousands of years ago when a huge meteorite rushed from the depths of space and plunged to earth at a speed of thousands of kilometres an hour. The terrible impact smashed a circular hole in the bedrock. The resulting crater is 854 metres across and 61 metres deep, the second largest in the world. Hundreds of kilometres to the southwest is another rock formation which draws the crowds. The Wave Rock, near Hyden, is a towering, 15 metre tall granite monolith which has been eroded by wind and water until it has assumed the shape of a gracefully curved breaker of the type loved by surfers.

But perhaps the greatest, and most famous, natural wonder of Western Australia is not as interesting as the Wolf Creek Crater, nor as beautiful as the Wave Rock. In fact it is terribly boring. What makes the Nullarbor Plain so famed is its sheer size. The flat, treeless plain stretches across more land than the entire state of Victoria and is one of the most inhospitable areas on the continent. This vast limestone plateau is riddled with caves, some of which contain remarkable natural stalactite and stalagmite formations. Across the plain runs the Trans-Australia Railway. Due to the extraordinary flatness of the region the engineers were able to lay the tracks in a straight line for 483 kilometres, the longest straight stretch of line in the world.

Another great route across the deserts of Western Australia is the 1,600 kilometre long Canning Stock Route. This track was surveyed in 1906 by A.W. Canning and for decades was used to transport cattle from Arnhem Land to the railhead at Wiluna. Modern means of transportation have long since rendered the route obsolete, the water holes have become derelict and the track difficult to follow. Even so, some specialised holiday firms organise expeditions to view the terrible heart of the Great Sandy Desert.

The more fertile areas of the state are not so abundant in mineral wealth, but they were the first to be settled by the migrants as they struggled to scratch a living from the soil. The site of the original settlement on the Swan River has long since been built over, but the type of land that Captain Stirling and his band of settlers found can be seen in many southwestern parts of the state. Sheep and wheat are the most important agricultural products in the area. Over 3 million hectares of land are given over to the production of wheat and the yield is around twenty bushels per hectare. Though the rate of production is not very high the farms are highly mechanised and farmers can enjoy a standard of living comparable to their city cousins. The sheep population of the state is around 35 million but unlike other states, wool is not the only product. Many of the sheep are bred for meat, indeed combined beef and lamb exports rival those of wool. In the northernmost areas of the state more emphasis is placed on grazing than in the southwestern part. Here farms are far larger than further south, some extending over some half million hectares or more. Unfortunately, the land is far less productive, with an average capacity of one sheep per eight hectares. In between these two relatively small, agricultural areas stretches the vast interior: the Great Sandy Desert, Great Victoria Desert and the Gibson Desert, which together with the barren hills of the west form a vast barrier to agriculture.

The great forests of the southwestern area are a vital asset of the state. Over 3 million hectares have been declared State Forests and are managed on the principle of sustained yield, thus each tree felled is replaced with another and the area of forest never diminishes. Along the coast fishing is an important money-spinner, exports of crayfish, or rock lobster, to the United States alone are worth many millions of dollars a year. Further to the north the pearling industry continues to flourish, though the pearling luggers have now been replaced by a cultured-pearl industry in Kuri Bay.

In the far southwest of the state stands the bustling capital of Perth, now the proud home of the America's Cup. The 'sunshine city' of Perth has come a long way since Captain Stirling arrived on an alien shore with his intrepid band of colonists. Today, the settlement has grown into a city throbbing with life and reflects well the prosperity of Western Australia. Indeed, the city is the hub and nerve centre of the whole state. Of the 1.3 million inhabitants of Western Australia over 900,000 live in or near their capital city. Perth is the most remote capital city in the world, being some 2,700 kilometres from Adelaide; the nearest other city of any size. Until 1970 there was only a single railway and a collection of dirt roads and

Facing page: Wave Rock *bottom* and Hippo's Yawn *top,* near Hyden.

ANZ
SAVINGS BANK AGENT
Hallmark Cellars
EMU EXPORT LAGER
DAILY NEWS
The Western Mail
OPEN

SELF SERVICE STORE
DELI
PITS
STORES
ESTD 1938
CENTRAL BUTCHERS
FILMS POSTCARDS
STORE and DELICATESSEN
MEALS & SNACKS
FURNITURE & FLOORCOVERINGS
FRUIT & VEGIES

tracks to connect the city with the eastern states. In that year the Eyre, or Great Eastern, Highway was completed across the Nullarbor Plain to Adelaide, and it is hoped that the Great Northern Highway to Darwin will soon be metalled.

This isolation has shaped the character and history of the city. The settlers had to be hardy and independent, able to make their own way in the world. Perth was proclaimed a city in 1856 and rapidly began to assume the role of the 'elegant city of Australia', a role it continued to play when it was made a lord mayoralty in 1929 and which persists to the present day. The city, together with the state, was largely ignored by the rest of the world, but prosperity and growth came with the discoveries of gold in the 1890s. The increasing agricultural and mineral exports which flowed through the city necessitated the improvement of Fremantle Harbour in 1901, which in turn stimulated increased exports. Today, Perth is not only accessible by road, rail and sea but also by air, via the large and impressive international airport.

Although the city is a major industrial centre, the heavy industries are concentrated in the suburbs of Fremantle, Welshpool and Kwinana. Prosperity relies on steel, aluminium and nickel; paint, plaster, cement and rubber, as well as petroleum refineries and food-processing plants.

Perth enjoys a wonderful climate. Straddling the blue waters of the Swan River – the natural habitat of the black swan – it enjoys a sea breeze which rises from Fremantle and cools the population on hot summer afternoons. The excellent climate makes all kinds of outdoor sports popular. Sailing is a passion with some people, which has resulted in the city's yacht club winning the sport's most prestigious trophy, and those not in boats can surf, swim or simply enjoy the sun and the splendid white, sandy beaches. Other favourite sports include hockey, cricket, bowls and tennis. Winter sports include "Australian Rules" football: a game with machismo. The post-war migration accounts for the existence of soccer, too. For others there is basketball, speedboat and car racing. It is all there for the taking!

The University of Western Australia is responsible for developing a mechanical sheepshearing machine, which can equal a man's time of three minutes. There is also a technical college, two teachers' training colleges and some private colleges. Perth has both Anglican and Roman Catholic cathedrals, and several historic buildings: the Barracks Arch, His Majesty's Theatre, the Town Hall with its clock tower, the Old Asylum, the Old Mill and Government House dating back to 1863.

The state of Western Australia is still 'The Frontier State'; a state of scattered homesteads, vast distances and great potential. The huge, newly-discovered deposits of minerals place Western Australia on the brink of dynamic growth, while its natural splendours and beautiful buildings truly make it 'The unique Australian state'.

Previous pages Pemberton and *insets* Manjimup and the fire lookout at Diamond Tree.

Facing page: beaches near Wyadup *top* and Yallingup *bottom*.

Overleaf Bunbury and *inset* its Catholic cathedral.

BANK
COMMONWEALTH
Sherry's
PHARMACY
BOOTMAKERS
Dinks
Coke
TEEDE
Barr & Standley
Miss Boyanup

AMPOL
AMPOL
M.B.A.
BUILDING INFOR
CENTRE
chemist

PARMELIA HILTON

State Capital of Western Australia, the sunshine city of Perth enjoys a wonderful climate. Straddling the blue waters of the Swan River – the natural habitat of the black swan – it is situated 19km above the port of Fremantle, which opens into the Indian Ocean. From here arises a sea breeze, 'the Fremantle doctor', which cools the population of 925,000 on hot summer afternoons.

It was in the early nineteenth century that the British, anxious about the intentions of the United States and France, decided to settle on the western coast of Australia and to claim the entire continent as their own. The move was no doubt prompted by recent colonial wars in India and America. These series of wars had their roots in the fact that both Britain and France had established colonies near to each other. The wars had been expensive in lives and money and the British Government was determined that the same situation should not develop in the potentially profitable land of Australia.

Until the 1820s Britain had only claimed the eastern part of the continent and even there the settlements were very small. In 1827, Captain James Stirling sailed along the western coast of Australia, charting the seas and looking for a good site for settlement. He returned with such glowing reports that several capitalist adventurers became interested in founding a colony. Two years later Captain Stirling returned and, on June 17 1829, read out a proclamation declaring that the whole western third of Australia belonged to Britain and that he was to be the first Lieutenant Governor. Though he only had 150 settlers with him, James Stirling was not in the least daunted by the prospect of settling an area ten times the size of Britain. Fremantle was founded at the mouth of the Swan River, to act as a port, and a slight hill was named Perth and declared to be the capital city. Within two years the population had increased tenfold to 1,500 souls, and the town has never looked back.

Today, the settlement has grown into a city bustling with life and reflects well the prosperity of Western Australia. It is in this context that it should be seen, serving 1.3 million people in an area nearly one-third the size of the continent. It is the most isolated capital in the world, with Adelaide 2,700 km to the east, along a road that was not even paved until 1976. This isolation shaped its history and character. Twelve thousand sea miles away from England, the early settlers had to be independent and hardy. They had to fight both the unforgiving land and harassment by Aborigines. Struggling together, the essential spirit of the people was forged true and strong. Elegant Perth was proclaimed a city in 1856 and a lord mayoralty in 1929, but it had a slow rate of growth until a small Irish tramp discovered one of the richest reefs of gold ore in the world. The gold was deep in the interior around the Coolgardie-Kalgoorlie area. From 1890 onwards thousands of hopefuls poured into the state and gold poured out. Perth, as the main port of the state, benefited enormously in wealth and population. Expansion was further aided by the telegraph link to Adelaide in 1877, and the improved Fremantle harbour of 1901. The trans-continental highway was completed in 1917 and today Perth is accessible by several highways, as well as by its international airport.

Although the city is a major industrial centre, the heavy industries are concentrated in Fremantle, Welshpool and Kwinana. Prosperity relies on steel, aluminium and nickel; paint, plaster, cement and rubber, as well as petroleum refineries and food-processing plants. The mineral wealth of Western Australia pours into Perth; there are huge deposits of iron in the state, as well as diamonds, bauxite, uranium and gold. There are also amongst the world's largest deposits of cobalt, vanadium, molybdenum, tantalum and chrome – the so-called strategic metals. The state is not only rich in mineral wealth; agriculture also plays a vital role in the economy. The land around Perth itself is rich and fertile, producing a wide range of crops. Even the drier land in the far north produces its share of wealth in the form of wool and beef.

Facing page Perth from Kings Park.

Overleaf Perth city centre.

PARMELIA HILTON

AMP AMP
City Arcade
BOANS LIMITED MANUFACTURERS BOANS LIMITED IMPORTERS

National Bank
AUSTRALIAN CORNER
AUSTRALIAN CORNER
BOANS

AMP AMP

MYER

CRAFTS

The excellent climate makes all kinds of outdoor sports popular. Sailing is a passion with some people and those not in boats can surf, swim or laze in the sun on the white, sandy beaches. Other favourite sports include hockey, cricket, bowls and tennis. Winter sports include "Australian Rules" football: a game with machismo. The post-war immigration accounts for the existence of soccer too. For others there is basketball, speedboat and car racing. It is all there for the taking!

Perth has been most fortunate in preserving its natural heritage. John Septimus Roe was the first surveyor general of the colony, and he was responsible for the setting aside of land for the public. He also banned the felling of trees on Mount Eliza. The result of his work is King's Park: a thousand acres of natural bushland overlooking the city and a source of much civic pride. Here is the War Memorial, where you may stand humbled before the obelisk to those who died in distant, foreign lands, so far from the peace and beauty of these sylvan paths. Not too far away there is also Yanchep Park, Queen's Park, Hyde Park and the John Forrest National Park. Just 20km offshore there is the holiday resort of Rottnest Island, home of the quokka. Doctors have discovered that this small marsupial has the ability to regenerate its muscle tissue when injected with massive doses of vitamin E. This may lead towards a cure for muscular dystrophy.

The University of Western Australia is resposible for developing a mechanical sheepshearing machine, which can equal a man's time of three minutes. There is also a technical college, two teachers' training colleges and some private colleges. Perth has both Anglican and Roman Catholic cathedrals, and several historic buildings: the Barracks Arch, His Majesty's Theatre, the Town Hall with its clock tower, the Old Asylum, the Old Mill and Government House dating back to 1863.

Perth is still at the frontier of a vast land, where children learn from the Schools of the Air and medical care is a visit from the flying doctor. Tempered by a history of struggle, the city stands gracefully, embracing a golden people of vibrant energy.

Facing page the Carrillion Centre in Perth.

Overleaf the city centre of Perth.

AMP
Elders

ROYAL
QANTAS

Above a gnarled tree stands watch over a park in Fremantle, Perth's port. Many of the important buildings in the city are surrounded by gardens of great beauty. *Far left and facing page, bottom* the neo-Gothic Catholic cathedral which stands amid trees and shrubs in Victoria Square while the gardens *facing page, top* lie before the Parliament Buildings. The strange Ore Obelisk *left*, which is to be found in Stirling Gardens, was erected to mark the arrival of the millionth inhabitant of Western Australia. *Overleaf* the centre of Perth.

CityMutual
Legal
General

SEC
R&I
GRAND CENTRAL PRIVATE HOTEL
NEW
30's

National Bank
IMPERIAL
PELLS SURPLUS
SANYO
AUSTRALIAN CORNER

Barrack Street *left and facing page* runs beside the central shopping mall, as does Murray Street *above* and William Street *below.* The Mall is an area of central Perth where vehicles are prohibited and pedestrians can shop in peace and quiet. The Mall includes a section of Hay Street where many large stores and small shops line its streets. *Top left* London Court. *Overleaf* Perth from Kings Park.

R&I
HOTEL
VISIONHIRE
KITCHEN
HUNGRY JACKS

CityMutual
CityMutual
AMP
AMP
PARMELIA HILTON

Located in the pleasant suburb of Crawley, the University of Western Australia *these pages* is the main seat of learning in the state. *Above and below* Winthrop Hall. *Overleaf* the scenes of jubilation which greeted the return of Alan Bond with the America's Cup in 1983 (picture by Michael Coyne/Talentbank).

AMP
ROYAL
AUSTRALIAN EAGLE
QANTAS
AUSTRALIA

GRIFFIN
ROOM WITH A VIEW
WABS

Though Fremantle *these pages* is often overshadowed by its larger neighbour, it has much to offer resident and visitor alike. The Round House Gaol *facing page, bottom,* a grim reminder of days gone by, stands alongside the High Street *left and facing page, top.* The magnificent buildings of the Market *far left,* the Harbour *above,* the Museum *top right* and Saint Patrick's Catholic Church *top left* are all based on European architectural styles.

FREMANTLE MUNICIPAL TRAMWAYS
STOP
TICKET

York *these pages* is the oldest inland town in the state, dating from 1830. Its main street is lined with an impressive array of historic buildings.

BOOKS
SOUTH ST
GIVE WAY

CENTRAL
1907
BUILDINGS
YORK TOURIST BUREAU
THE CRAFT SHOP
MILK BAR
LAND & REAL ESTATE
XPY-730

The great gold cities of Western Australia, Coolgardie and Kalgoorlie, both commemorate their pioneers in street names. The building seen *right* stands on Coolgardie's Bayley Street. It was Arthur Bayley and his friend William Ford who discovered gold here. Kalgoorlie named its main street *remaining pictures* after Paddy Hannan, who stumbled across the Golden Mile in 1893.

KELLY'S
CHEMIST
emists
BUTCHERS
WATCHMAKER
ANZ BANK
Coolgardie
Perth
Hicks
HOME FURNISHERS

HOCKING & Co LIMITED
THE MINER & WESTERN ARGUS OFFICES
Hocking & Co Pty Ltd.
Kalgoorlie Miner
EXCHANGE HOTEL

Unlike most other towns of the Gold Rush days, Kalgoorlie has survived into the late twentieth century with a promising future. Over a thousand tonnes of gold have been wrested from the earth in this area and it is still being found. Many of the grandest buildings in the city date from the boom days; the Town Hall *above* was built in 1908. Another great feature of the old times is the pipeline that runs a staggering 597 kilometres from Perth to provide the thirsty miners with water. The peak population of 30,000 has now fallen to some 20,000, but the city is now an established centre. Gold mining continues, of course, but the pastoral potential of the surrounding countryside is now being realised. *Overleaf* the Pinnacles.

Kalgoorlie Miner
EXCHANGE
HOTEL

MEALS

These pages Kalbarri National Park lies some 150km north of Geraldton and is noted for its coloured rock cliffs, the banded appearance of which is due to beds of red sandstone that underlie the region. Over thousands of years, the whole coastal plain has been uplifted by some 200 metres, creating the inland gorges and coastal cliffs.

Previous pages the beach near Kalbarri. The Hamersley Range *these pages* stands at the heart of the mineral-rich Pilbara. Throughout the area, towns such as Tom Price and Paraburdoo exist as bases for iron ore mining. Thousands of tonnes of rock are ripped from the ground each year and loaded on giant trains for transport to the coast. But the region's chief attraction for tourists is its remarkable scenery. Plunging chasms drop hundreds of metres to almost dry river beds; Tinto Gorge *below left* is a striking example. But most dramatic of all are the colours: vivid hues of red and mauve, interspersed with the golden bands of dry spinifex, draw thousands of tourists here each year. *Overleaf* landscape near Kununurra.

John Stokes of Her Majesty's Ship *Beagle* viewed the scene before his eyes with obvious satisfaction. The inlet was deep and would one day provide safe anchorage for many a proud, tall-masted ship. It was the year 1839 and the name given to this natural harbour by the men of the *Beagle* was Port Darwin. This was in honour of the naturalist and scientist Charles Darwin, who had previously spent five years aboard the vessel, from December 1831 to October 1836.

In 1864, the first coastal town in the Northern Territory was established at the mouth of the Adelaide River. The name given to the settlement was Palmerston, but a terrible wet season the following year meant that it had to be abandoned. However, a party led by William Goydor, Surveyor-General of South Australia, set up a base some fifty kilometres east of the present site of Darwin, at Adam Bay. He surveyed the surrounding area, looking all the while for a permanent site, and chose Port Darwin as the most suitable place.

Although this new town was officially called Palmerston, too, it was generally known as Port Darwin to save confusion with the nearby settlement that had previously been abandoned. In 1911, control of the Northern Territory passed from South Australian to Australian Commonwealth administration and Palmerston was officially given the name of Darwin.

As well as being a transportation and communications centre of considerable importance, Darwin is particularly noted for its international airport and for being the terminus for shipping on the east-west coastal routes. It is the end of the railway from Birdum, 509 kilometres to the southeast, and of the Stuart Highway from Alice Springs, which lies over 1,500 kilometres away. This road was to achieve importance during the Second World War as Darwin became a strategic centre. A total of 1,534 kilometres of 'The Track' were sealed to aid ease of transportation to Australia's northern outpost.

It was not only strategic reasons which helped Darwin to develop. Like many other places in Australia, the discovery of minerals played an important role at several periods in its history. In the 1870s, the population reached 10,000 during a gold rush to the district of Pine Creek, but this boom soon came to an end. In the early 1950s, uranium ore was discovered at nearby Rum Jungle.

Other discoveries in the Northern Territory led to Darwin's growth as the outlet for these natural resources. In 1965-66, mining of iron ore was commenced at Frances Creek and at Mt Bundey. Manganese ores were also being exploited at the same time on the island of Groote Eylandt. Between 1969-70, over 1,000,000 tonnes of iron ore was exported to Japan. The United States, Europe and Japan took the manganese ore to the value of $10,800,000. Gold and copper were mined mainly at Tennant Creek. Lead and zinc deposits were found near the McArthur River and at Woodcutters, near Darwin. Oil and gas deposits are now being found and developed. Today, Darwin enjoys the benefits of a bonanza of minerals and seems economically secure as a direct result.

Darwin is one of Australia's most cosmopolitan cities, with people from some forty-seven different racial and cultural backgrounds rubbing shoulders. Since its earliest days, Chinese people have formed one of the largest of the immigrant groups, however, Timorese and Southeast Asians fleeing from strife have recently formed one of the latest peoples to find shelter in Australia. Indeed, over the years, Darwin has often been the first glimpse that people have had of their new-found home. Some people never get any further, enchanted as they are by this city nestled under the tropical sun.

As in dress, so in life style, Darwin is an open-necked city where a relaxed approach is still the vogue. As both the gateway to Australia in the north and as an outlet for the mineral wealth of the Northern Territory, the future of this city seems to be assured.

Facing page, top central Darwin. *bottom* the Law Courts, Darwin.

T&G
TOWN AUTO WHOLESALERS

Darwin: *right, top and facing page, top* Smith Street, *above* St Mary's Star of the Sea Cathedral and *facing page, bottom* the casino at Mindil Beach.

ANNIVERSARY
CELEBRATIONS
AMPHITHEATRE
CONCERT
BUSHWACKERS
and BULLAMAKANKA
SAT. 25TH. June
WOOLWORTHS

Darwin has a great mix of buildings old, new and exotic. *Right and above right* the Joss House at the Chinese Temple. *Above* the maximum security cells of the Fannie Bay Gaol Museum.

Top the Reserve Bank of Australia. *Facing page, top* the luxurious, modern casino which overlooks the Timor Sea at Mindil Beach. *Facing page, bottom* Government House.

S.W.L. 25 TON
1981
ROAD
TRAIN
HALKITIS BROS

Darwin: *top* the artillery museum at East Point, *above* antennae outside ABC in Cavenagh Street, *right* a ship at Fort Hill Wharf and *facing page, top and bottom* unloading sulphur at Stokes Hill Wharf.

Beyond the Great Dividing Range and the coastal rim of Australia, lies the "outback".

This vast land is still a frontier, both physically and in spirit. It is an area of adventure and myth, holding echoes of the Aboriginal "Dreamtime".

The first venture into the centre of Australia from Adelaide was the abortive expedition of 1844, headed by Captain Charles Sturt, who is quoted as having said that it was: "a landscape which never changes but for the worse". The Burk and Wills expedition of 1860 left Melbourne on 20th August to cross the mysterious, red interior of the continent. Their party took with them 23 horses, 25 camels and 3 drays. Their 21 tons of stores and equipment included 37 firearms and 60 gallons of rum. Although they achieved their aim by reaching swampland around the Gulf of Carpentaria in February 1861, tragedy awaited on the return journey when Burke and Wills died of malnutrition.

Visitors to the outback are struck by its heat, brilliant light, the red earth and the eucalyptus trees. The English novelist, D.H. Lawrence, was appalled by "the vast, uninhabited land and by the grey charred bush...so phantom-like, so ghostly, with its tall, pale trees and many dead trees, like corpses". However, to native Australians the land appears more friendly and familiar.

The centre of Australia is unique. Here, the outback is one of the last places on earth where the raw works of nature remain untouched by man. The limitless horizons are hazed by the heat and rearing up from the "Red Centre", with its sunlit plain and shimmering mirages, is the world's largest monolith – Ayers Rock. Nine kilometres in circumference and 348 metres high, it is only the tip of a huge rock massif which tipped on its side aeons ago. It is an awesome sight as the sun's rays paint its sides a kaleidoscope of colours from brown to brilliant red, purple and black. Sacred to the Aborigines, there are legends depicted in rock paintings in galleries at its base.

Thirty-two kilometres west of Ayers Rock are a series of domes rising from the arid plain, together forming the Olgas. Deposited, like The Rock, 600 million years ago during the Cambrian period, these rocks also change colour with the sweep of the sun's path. Both *Uluru* (The Rock) and *Katatjuta* (the Olgas) feature stongly in the lives of the Yankuntjatjara and Pitjandjara tribes. The Ayers Rock-Mt Olga National Park covers an area of 126,132 hectares, about 450 kilometres southwest of Alice Springs. For the adventurous, access is by gravelled road, or else there are air tours which operate out of Alice Springs.

To the east and west of this town are found the Macdonnell Ranges; among the oldest mountains in the world. They consist of hard quartzite ridges wandering over the sun-baked landscape for over 300 kilometres. Within the area covered by the Ranges are small, though fascinating, parks and reserves. For many years the only supply link that Alice Springs had with the south was the camel trains with their Afghan drivers. Nowadays diesel trains make the journey into the heartland.

Vast and solitary, with ever-retreating horizons, the outback is an unforgiving land which does not make allowance for weaknesses. Human life is an intrusion barely tolerated. This is one of the least populated areas of the world, many families living on isolated cattle stations where pastoral land is necessarily reckoned in hectares per animal. But the breathtaking beauty of this harsh land is what keeps people here. Strange rock shapes, gnarled by nature's untamed forces, cover the land; the brilliant plumage of an exotic bird flashes past the eye; the vast vista of space and light, with an intense ultramarine sky above, creates a dome of solitude.

Because neighbours may be several hundred kilometres away, there has been formed a

Previous pages Fogg Dam bushlands, west of Darwin.

Facing page Twin Falls in Kakadu National Park.

special, unique lifestyle for these isolated people. Horsemanship is the outback skill of choice, although the four-wheel-drive vehicle is now the true workhorse of the grazier and cattleman. The rodeo or race meeting attracts a far-flung audience as families fly there in their own planes. The Royal Flying Doctor Service provides medical care for these people, this being an Australian innovation which has taken root in other countries, such as in the more remote parts of Canada. The radio and telephone have also helped to reduce the remoteness and loneliness of this way of life. Yet, despite the benefits of modern technology the outback is still a place of mystery which, for the unwary or careless, can spell disaster.

The outback is a harsh mistress who in time of drought will scour stockland with blown sand. However, unexpected rain will allow the desert lands to reveal a myriad wild flowers, dazzling the observer with their variety and riotous colours. The fauna of the outback is also part of Australia's great natural heritage. The once-ubiquitous kangaroo is symbolic of the family of marsupials that flourishes on the island continent, safe from the competition of superior mammals. Here can also be seen the koala, the wombat, the echidna and the platypus. The bird life is also famous for the emu, lyrebird, parrot, cockatoo and bower-bird. Although there is beauty, there's danger, too, for the person who meets the tiger snake or the red-backed spider. Safe in their natural havens, miles from human habitation, these animals thrive in their outback habitat. Only careless deprivation through man's relentless technological expansion imperils the natural inheritance of millennia.

Because of scarcity of water and pasture in the lonely vastness of the outback, stockmen and their herds are often on the move in search of fertile land. Despite recurrent droughts and hazards, such as bush fires, production of beef and wool remains at a high level. Rangeland farming, combined with other changes wrought by man, has radically altered parts of the outback ecosystem. But, fortunately, the sheer size of the land has helped absorb the impact made by modern man. The introduction of national parks, sanctuaries and reserves has helped stem the tide of man-made change, and the unique diversity of fauna and flora in the outback will continue to be a rich asset for generations of people yet to come.

The archetypal outback Australian rides tall in the saddle, a sunburnt and rugged individual. However, four out of five Australians live in cities. The outback and its way of life then becomes an ideal that echoes frontier values and speaks of simplicity of action, room to breathe and adventure, far removed from urbanity and bureaucracy. This then is the dual nature of the outback – a land of solitary beauty and a vision for dreamers.

Facing page the thermal pool at the Mataranka Homestead.

Tennant Creek *these pages,* with its prestigious Civic Centre *facing page, bottom,* owes its relative prosperity to the presence of gold, silver and other scarce minerals, in the surrounding hills.

MANS WORLD
BETTING SHOP
TENNANT CREEK
HOTEL

These pages the truckers are a colourful group of characters who regularly cross the outback. *Above and facing page* road trains at Dunmarra. *Top* the bar and reception area of the Mataranka Homestead. *Right and centre right* along the Stuart Highway.

RAILEX
MACK
ROAD
TRAIN
251·153

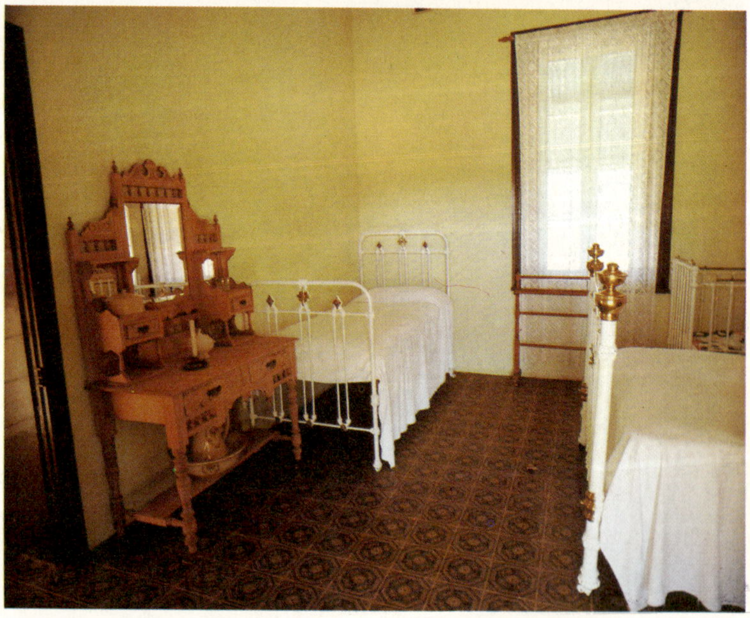

The Old Telegraph Station *these pages*, near Alice Springs, is now an historic site. The Overland Telegraph Line crossed the Macdonnell Ranges through Heavitree Gap to reach the town. Today, there is an animal compound there, where emus and kangaroos can be seen. The town of Alice Springs was surveyed in 1889 and was declared to be a town in 1890. However, it was then named Stuart – the town did not acquire its present name until later.

TELEGRAPH
OFFICE

Previous pages the town of Alice Springs. *These pages* the Dreamtime Tour operates out of Alice Springs and offers a chance to see some traditional techniques that have been employed by Aborigines for millennia: a man displays his prowess with a spear and boomerang; a woman makes a fire to cook some tasty witchetty grubs, found among a bush's roots.

These pages the Palm Valley Fauna and Flora Reserve. It includes not only the small tourist area known as Palm Valley, but also hundreds of kilometres of twisting gorges cut by the Finke River into the Krichauff and James Ranges. The palms, *Livistona mariae,* were found by the explorer Ernest Giles in 1872. To explore the area fully one has to resort to a four-wheel-drive vehicle, or else hike to see this most beautiful nature reserve.

These pages Standley Chasm, in the West Macdonnell Ranges, is a little over 50 kilometres from Alice Springs. This high, sheer-walled feature, set amid the rugged terrain of the Macdonnells, is a splendid example of nature's work. Being so narrow and tall, the sun only penetrates the crevice when it has climbed near to its noonday position. Then the walls turn from burnt umber to flaming red as the sun's rays flash down to the heart of the chasm. There is only limited vegetation to be found here, although gum trees find sustenance in this oasis amid the harsh terrain of the Centre. In places, crystal clear water is found, refreshing throats – and minds – accustomed to arid outback and remorseless sun.

Both Ayers Rock *top, right, above, facing page, bottom and overleaf* and the Olgas *facing page, top* present kaleidoscopic, transient colours to the observer. Set in the heart of the Red Centre, the sun's rays impart the quality of incandescence to their bare stone surfaces in shades of flaming red. Both rock massifs are the focus for much Aboriginal Dreamtime legend.

At the western end of Ayers Rock *these pages* – *Uluru* as it is called by the Aborigines – visitors can take the long climb to the top along the imposing ridgeline. On the summit, a lonely cairn marks the highest point. The reward, besides the climb itself, is the panoramic splendour which unfolds as height is gained. When standing upon the very pinnacle of the monolith one can see the vast sweep of the outback. This is the land of the Never-Never. For endless aeons nature has shaped the land and the land shaped its inhabitants; the Aborigines. Then white men came and boldly struck out into the burning vastness of the outback. The challenge is still there for the adventurous in spirit.

Overleaf the rounded, chasm-split domes of the Olgas.